Southern Wisdom

AN INSIDER'S GUIDE
TO SAYINGS 'N' SUCH

EMILY WELCH

ROCK
POINT

· Dedication ·

For Patrice, Aud, and Mimi, the ultimate
Southern hostesses in my life that I've been
lucky enough to learn from.
I hope that I'm able to impart half the wisdom
you've taught me to my Audrey.

CONTENTS

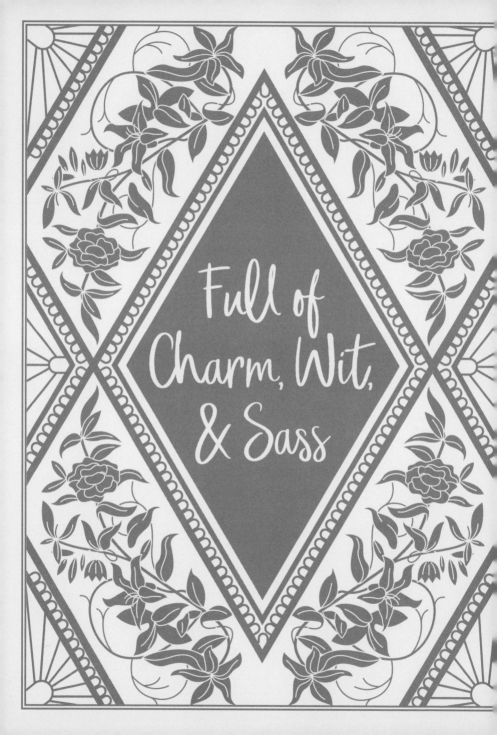

Full of
Charm, Wit,
& Sass

· Introduction ·

WHEN CONVERSATIONS IN OUR FAMILY TURN TO OUR Northern friends, my husband always tells our kids, "There's a reason people don't retire North." He's referring to their extremely cold weather or the fact that their food doesn't have the same "spice" as ours does—things Southerners really do not handle well. People also think everyone who retires in the South does it for the warmer weather, the humidity, or the beautiful golf courses in Florida, but they would be wrong too. The reason is simple: this wonderful place we call home is full of it…in more ways than one. Full of what? Full of people who are hospitable while also offering a hidden but lovingly sweet jab at the recipient's expense. Southerners, as a people, are full of charm, wit, and a true knowing of how to turn each and every day into a celebration. It's the motto we live by. But at the same time, we contradict and twist everything we say, just for a laugh. We're full of sweetness, sass, and our own unique blend of *je ne sais quoi*. The South is intoxicating, engaging, and, most of all, it's a way of life.

In the South, we have our parades, parties, and cotillions on top of hurricanes, secrets, and voodoo spells. These things make us different and beloved and create the allure that is the unforgettable Southern United States. I want you to sit down with a big glass of sweet tea and consider this book a nice firm handshake and hug, welcoming you to our party with open arms. When you're done reading, I hope you look at the calendar and plan a trip to Mardi Gras, Jazz Fest, BBQ and Blues Fest, or any SEC football game in the fall. Please call your local travel agent and come on down. We'd love to see ya!

Big Ole Families

My husband frequently jokes that he can't take me anywhere without meeting someone I'm related to. For example, when my husband brought me to watch an LSU football game (Geaux Tigers!) at his friend's house, I overheard a conversation and told him the woman just had to be from Broussard, Louisiana, based on her accent. My husband didn't believe me and laughed me off, and like *all* Southern women, I was happy to prove him wrong. I introduced myself and found out she was a second cousin I had never met. That's how it goes in the South—we're everywhere!

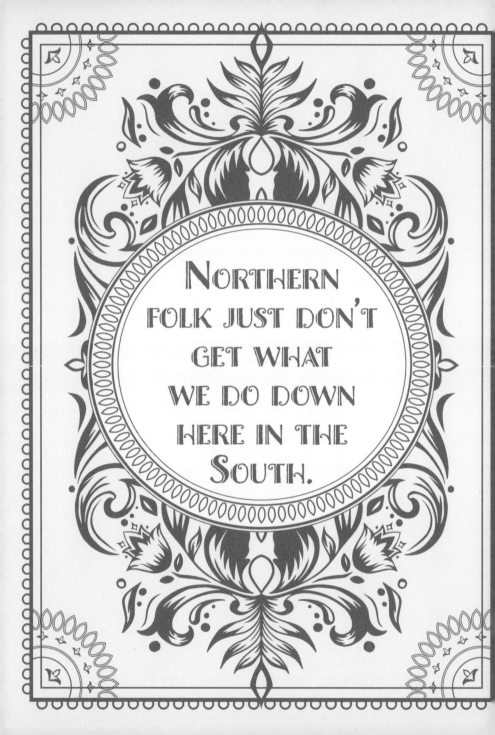

NORTHERN
FOLK JUST DON'T
GET WHAT
WE DO DOWN
HERE IN THE
SOUTH.

THE DISTINCTION BETWEEN NORTHERNERS IN THE
South and Southerners in the South is one that needs to be
made. Sure, we all love our families and enjoy get-togethers, but
life as a Southerner . . . well, it's just different. What makes us
different? Our vocabulary, our music, and our culture. Ask any
Northerner to translate "Southern speak," and they just can't!
For things that may be common in other parts of the country,
we make up our own words—we make it unique. Our music is
our own too. We love the accordion, the fiddle, and way down
in Cajun country, we even know how to rock a washboard! Our
lifestyle down here is one of a slower pace, something that
almost seems frowned upon up North. We enjoy speaking to
strangers we meet and consider everyone a friend.

GENERALLY, IN SOCIETY, IT IS AGREED UPON THAT there are three things you *never* discuss in public: money, politics, and religion. However, in the South, those are the things we *always* talk about. My fraternal grandmother, affectionately known as Big Girl Aud, used to always ask me about my friends: "Who was their mama?" or "Who are their people?" Like most Southern grandmothers, Big Girl Aud knew *a lot* of people and chances are, she knew their people too. That's the thing about Southerners: we are nosy, but for good reason. Southerners treat everyone like family. We want to make connections. We enjoy finding new friends and bringing them into the fold.

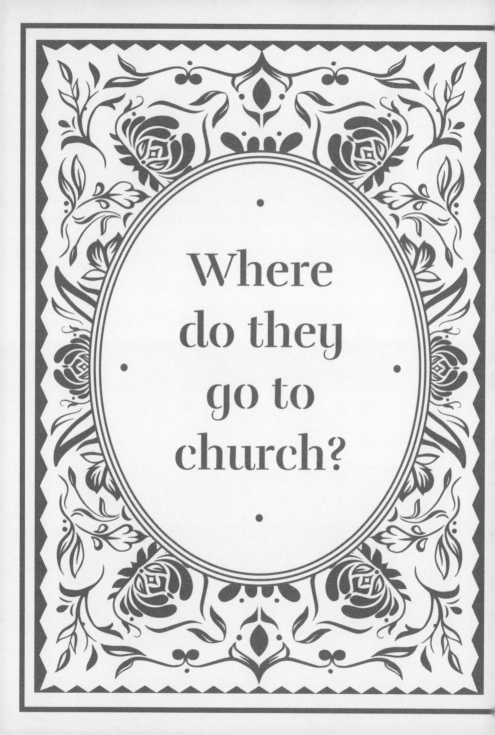

Where
do they
go to
church?

ALMOST AS IMPORTANT AS WHO SOMEONE IS related to is where they go to church. Before I go any further, talking about where you go to church is totally different than talking about religion. The question of your religion refers to your belief system, but where you go to church specifically means the building you visit at least once a week and who you see and converse with while you are there.

People who go to church together are considered one big family. Church is not only a way for people to find common ground religiously, but also how Southerners identify education. In the South, most churches have schools attached to them, so where you go to church is often where you went to school. High school is usually much more important here than college because of football. (Football in the South is its own religion—that still reigns supreme.)

GRANDMOTHERS, IN THE SOUTH, ARE USUALLY THE head of the family, the teachers, the helpers, and the main storytellers. They know everyone, and more importantly, they remember . . . everything! By nature, they hold a special reverence in the South. They are loving, kind, thoughtful, and will put you in your place quicker than you can blink! You can almost bet all these quick-witted phrases from the South everyone loves were created by someone's grandmother. They lead by example. And if they know someone who's related to your family, they're sure to share a funny or embarrassing story, followed by lots of laughter and cocktails.

"

Call your
grandmother.

"

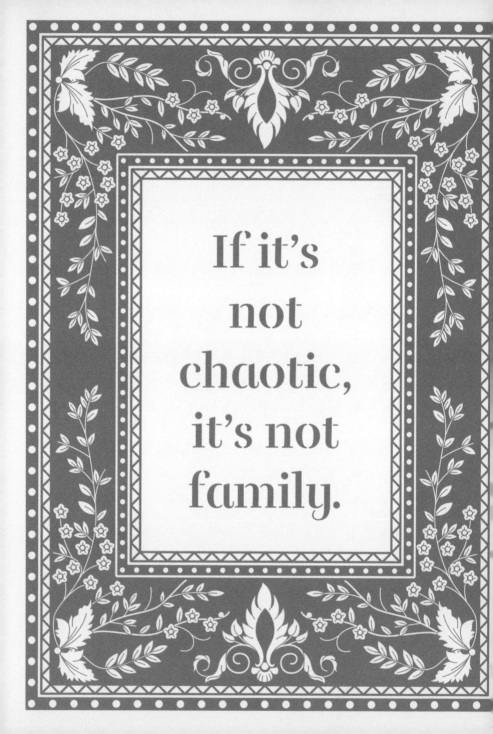

If it's
not
chaotic,
it's not
family.

ONE UNIQUE ASPECT OF THE SOUTHERN FAMILY
deals with members who are not actually blood related. It is
a very common occurrence in the South to call friends family
names, such as aunt and uncle, especially family friends.
Perhaps it's also because our families tend to be so large, who
is really going to notice if we throw in a few extra people? Like
many Southerners, I have aunts and uncles whom I'm not
actually related to, but I've grown up calling them Aunt This
and Uncle That. I was probably eight or so before I truly realized
who was and was not a blood relative.

CHARTING FAMILY RELATIONSHIPS IS QUITE important to Southerners. We have separate libraries and even entire conferences devoted solely to genealogy. Genealogy is tracked by our ornate and beautiful graveyards and headstones. I remember growing up watching my mother and all my aunts pouring over huge binders for hours, overflowing with copies of newspaper clippings, birth certificates, wedding and cotillion announcements, and crudely hand-drawn charts of family trees going back to when our ancestors came to America. This was a favorite pastime for them at family gatherings. They enjoyed making connections of all the relatives, plotting the past and even the future of the family. Today, most of this research is easily found online or through send-off kits and cheek swabs, but I will treasure these binders and the handwritten charts because it is proof of the love of the family bond.

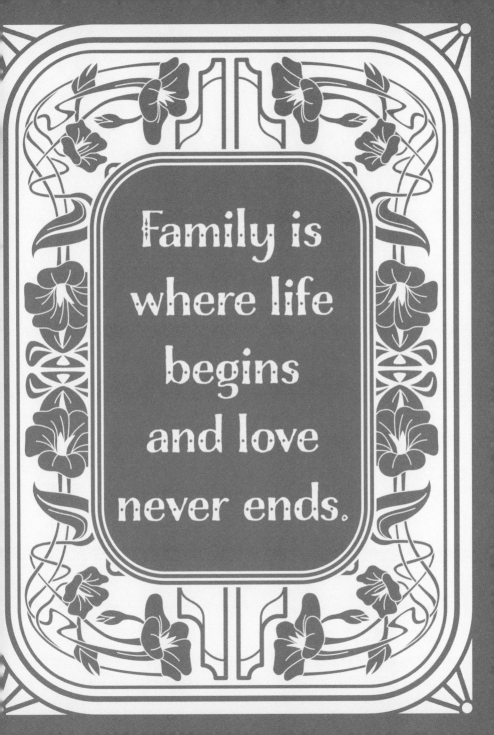

Family is
where life
begins
and love
never ends.

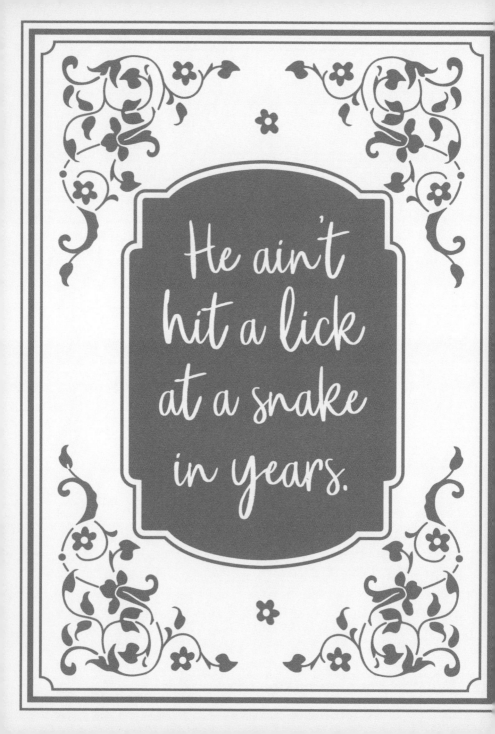

He ain't hit a lick at a snake in years.

IF YOU HEAR THIS SAYING, THEY'RE CALLING someone plain lazy. Every family has someone like this. (And lots of times it's usually a man.) This is someone who is so lazy they wouldn't hit a snake away if it crossed their path. Even if it was about to bite them, they wouldn't do nothing to stop it. I recommend doing your best not to become this person, but also to not find yourself with this person either. They're not the reliable type and probably not too much fun either. It's better to stick with the folks who know how to throw a party and have fun at one too.

• • ● • •

"ALL GET OUT" IS A PHRASE OF IMPORTANCE AND can have many uses in conversation depending on what you add with it. You can be tired as all get out, mad as all get out, or even surprised as all get out. Something can be funny or stupid as all get out. You can work this into everyday stories, most often ones about your family. Considering how much time we spend with them, there's always going to be a story or a person who elicits this level of emotion on any given day. Just make sure you state it with the accurate emotion it implies.

• • ● • •

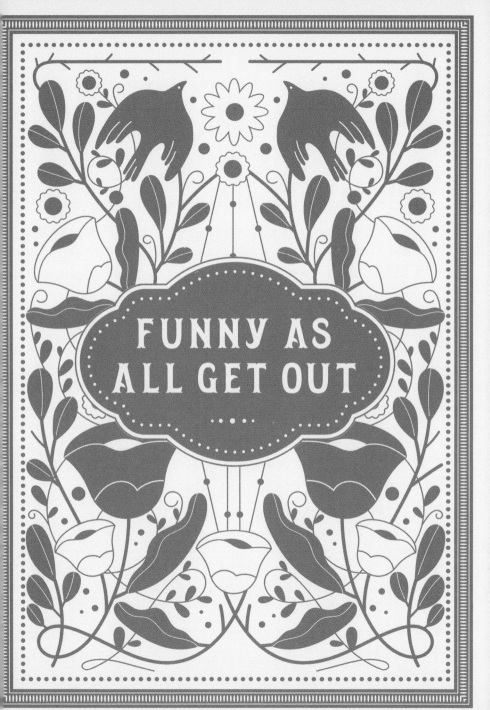

FUNNY AS
ALL GET OUT

She's gettin' above her raisin'.

WHEN YOU WANT TO CHANGE YOUR SOCIAL CLASS or where you come from, you're gettin' above your raisin'. Usually, someone says this as an insult when they don't believe a person is capable of moving up in the world. But it also can be used as a defense. One reason people stay in the South is to avoid their family members talking negatively once they're gone. We Southerners love being Southern, and if you decide to make a change, move away, and affiliate yourself with another culture, that could be seen as an insult to everyone you leave behind. This snobby phrase comes from a 1951 song by Earl Scruggs and was later covered by Ricky Skaggs.

THIS IS ONE OF THE MOST POPULAR SOUTHERN phrases. It's useful for many scenarios, including excitement, horror, surprise, and disgust. Anytime something shocking happens, you can say, "Oh, heavens to Betsy," and Southerners will understand that it almost knocked you all the way to heaven. Every well-mannered woman who proclaims this will also need to clutch her pearls or monogrammed handkerchief to get the desired effect. Just from that imagery alone, you can probably guess who in your life, or in the Southern family, would most often use this phrase.

HEAVENS TO BETSY

THAT

DOG

WON'T

HUNT.

WHEN FOLKS SAY A DOG WON'T HUNT, THEY MEAN he's not doing what he's paid to do. He was probably the laziest puppy in the litter. When he gets older, you'll probably find him lying around, basking in the sunshine on the front porch rather than prowling the pastures searching for critters that may invade his home. But while he's not doing much hard work, there's really no telling him off because he's just too darn cute to scold. This dog is often a family dog who has been around for so long that he gets away with anything these days—including doing nothing.

THIS PHRASE IS ALL ABOUT REDUNDANCY. IF SOMEONE is preachin' to the choir, it means they are trying to convince someone of something they already believe. Southerners are known for being long-winded, so when someone uses this phrase, it's a sign that they want us to stop while we're ahead because they already know or got it five sentences ago. The South is full of religion and churches, so a saying about a preacher just a talkin' and a talkin' is an easy one for us to comprehend.

Preachin' to the choir

MAMA'LL HAVE A DUCK FIT.

SIBLINGS OFTEN SAY THIS TO ONE ANOTHER when they know they have done something wrong. Say they accidentally broke one of grandma's nice plates, or they spilled something on the carpet, or the dog ate something that was prepared for supper. If mama is having a duck fit, she's madder than mad. She's angrier than a wet hen for sure and someone is to blame for it!

MANY PEOPLE IN THE SOUTH HAVE DEEP ROOTS HERE.
Their lineage goes back decades or even centuries, to the
first settling of the area sometimes. It's a place where
people set down their stones with no intention of picking
them up and moving away. And that means families in the
South are huge. For instance, most of my family lives in the
same city, with many only a block or even a couple of streets
away from each other. I have sixteen first cousins just on
one side. You can imagine how many I have today now that
we're all grown, married, and with families of our own. This
always made for huge holiday gatherings and the occasional
casual ones as well.

COMING FROM
A BIG FAMILY
MEANS
THERE IS
NEVER A DULL
MOMENT, NOR A
QUIET ONE.

Tricks for Passing as a Southerner

Welcome to the South, the world of sweet tea, dinner and supper, and large family get-togethers. We'll always welcome you with open arms, but these little tips will help you fit in just fine.

• • • • •

1. *Learn how to say and spell y'all correctly.* Down South, we always shorten "you all" to "y'all." We also spell it y'all not ya'll. Be sure to draw out those Ls. Otherwise, it's a dead giveaway that you're not really from here.

2. *Learn how to make the perfect biscuits.* Southerners love their biscuits and have them with almost every meal. The fluffier they are, the more you look like you belong here. So, get in the kitchen and start baking!

3. *Discover new family members you never knew you had.* Southerners often have large families, and if you want to pass as one of us, you'll need one too. If you don't have one, we also love tall tales, so make up some Aunt Pies and Uncle Sugs and even some knee-slapping stories to go with them. You'll be welcomed into the fold in no time.

4. *Write the perfect thank-you note.* Every Southern guest, male or female, knows the art of the thank-you note. Be sure to always send one after every gathering you're invited to. It's only polite.

5. *Throw in a properly timed "Bless your heart."* You've got to say it at least once, but you need to know *when*. This is our favorite veiled insult we're famous for, and if you can't seamlessly add it in conversation, we'll see right through your Southern mask—and you'll for sure be the next story shared that's accompanied with a "Bless their heart" after.

Natural Conditions

Years ago, I went to a design conference in Dallas, Texas, and used the following as my business mantra: "No matter what storm comes your way, always *laissez les bons temps rouler*." Whether it be after a huge storm hits, Mardi Gras falls on a cold winter's day, or an out-of-towner can't quite understand you because your accent is too thick, these are the natural conditions of life in the South. No matter what comes our way, we always look for the good. Or, like my daughter says, "Sometimes you just got to grit your teeth and go."

IF THE SOUTH IS FAMOUS FOR ONE SPECIFIC TYPE of weather, it would be hurricanes. Living close to large bodies of water, this is something we expect in the late summer and early fall. Every year, Southerners await the predicted number of storms and get to know the list of proposed names for said storms. These beasts can reach from Texas all the way over to the Carolinas and down to the tip of Florida. We fear them just as much as we celebrate them. New Orleans has a cocktail (the Hurricane), North Carolina has a hockey team (Carolina Hurricanes), and Miami has a football team (Miami Hurricanes) all in honor of these storms. But whenever the words "tropical storm" are uttered on the local news, Southerners rush to the grocery to load up on food, water, and, most importantly, liquor, leaving the shelves bare.

THE CLOSER TO THE GULF OF MEXICO YOU GET,
the higher the humidity. This warm weather and moisture-rich air is a great reason to move to the South. If you're not used to it, the first time you step out into the high heat and humidity can feel like you just got smacked in the face with a sauna. But once you get accustomed to it, your skin and hair will thank you. Moisture-rich environments are best for our bodies and just make you feel and look good. It's another thing we Southerners love about livin' in the South.

That ain't heat, that's humidity.

It's so cold, I saw a politician with his hands in his *own* pockets.

LUCKILY, OUR TIME WITH COLD WEATHER IS BRIEF in the South. Our friends up North can handle all the snow, but a half an inch of snow or ice will shut down an entire Southern city for a week, if not more. The coldest weather usually lands from January through February. Christmas and even Mardi Gras, depending on when it falls, are frequently celebrated while wearing shorts. But we put up with these cold temperatures because we know that right around the corner is spring: full of warm, beautiful weather and garden cocktail parties.

WHEN YOU SAY THIS, IT MEANS YOU HAVE A GOAL and you're on a mission. As long as there is nothing out of your control to stop you, you're going to accomplish it. Someone might say it if they're running late to an event, or if they're trying something new and don't have too much faith in themselves, or when they think something is a bad idea, but they're going to do it anyways. "If the Good Lord's Willing and the Creek Don't Rise" is also a country song by Jerry Reed but was made famous when it was recorded by Southern son Johnny Cash in 1958.

GOOD LORD
WILLIN'
THAT CREEK
WON'T RISE.

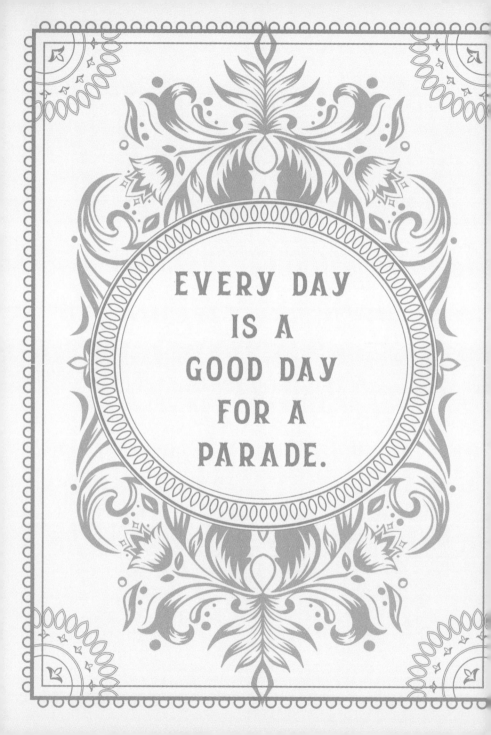

EVERY DAY
IS A
GOOD DAY
FOR A
PARADE.

IN THE SOUTH, WE LOVE TO BE OUTDOORS,
especially if it gives us a chance for eating, drinking, cooking,
hunting, or playing sports. We tend to celebrate events,
holidays, seasonal fruits and vegetables, and music with
a parade. The best high school bands and the local beauty
queens are brought out and put on floats flanked by music,
lights, glitter, and costumes. If you're lucky enough to attend
a parade in Louisiana, you'll be bombarded with lots of beads
and other throws. Mardi Gras—a huge event prepared year-
round with krewe members loading up on beads and throws
while decorating beautiful and brightly lit floats—may be the
most famous Southern celebration reaching from Louisiana
to Georgia.

THE REGULAR FOOTBALL SEASON STARTS IN LATE
August and runs through December. Our mild winters are
befitting incredible tailgating that can go on all day. I
remember when I was in college and my friends went out the
night before a game on campus to "stake their claim" and set
up tents and chairs for the next day. An abundance of goods is
prepped, beer is stocked, and ice chests are filled. Tailgating is
an art in the South. People devote countless hours to setting
up tents with satellite TVs, loading up tables with catered
food, and sometimes hanging a crystal chandelier from the
tents at the University of Mississippi. In the South, college
football is bigger than pro football mainly due to our lack of
pro teams. However, our high school football stadiums rival
college football stadiums up North.

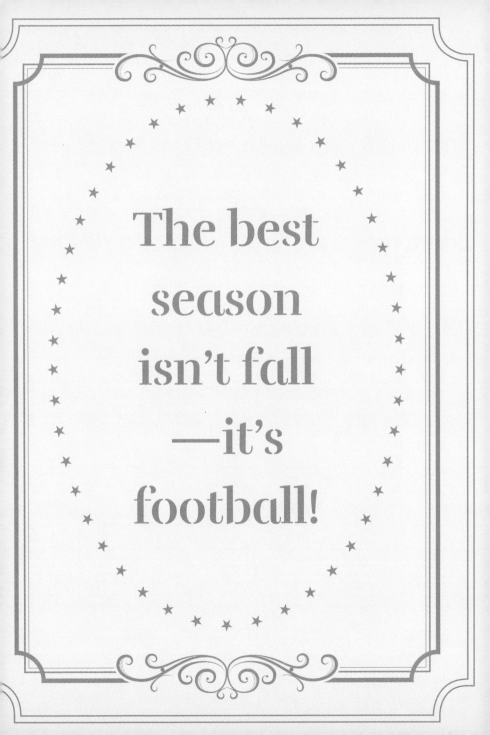

The best season isn't fall —it's football!

The
competition
is not just
on the
field.

SPEAKING OF ATTIRE, COORDINATING TEAM CLOTHING is huge in the South. I'm not talking about simple T-shirts with the team logo on them. I'm talking about actual dresses, tops, and jackets all made in college team colors. The fashion industry in the South has blossomed by creating dresses of purple and yellow, houndstooth scarves and belts, and jackets in an orange-checkered pattern. Saturday evenings in the South could be accompanied by our own postshow awards rating all the best-dressed people of the night. We also love to adorn our homes in our team colors, from bunting to flags to door hangers. We have team spirit, and we love to show it!

THIS FAMOUS PHRASE TRANSLATES TO, "NO MATTER what trying times come at you, always look for the good." It's used frequently in Louisiana, especially around Mardi Gras, and printed on countless cups, T-shirts, or anything that will stand still. It's a silver lining morale we live by. How many times have our people lost everything they have to a hurricane? Every time, the community picks each other up, rallies, and rebuilds. The cheery outlook that everyone you meet can use a hand is a part of our resilience and willingness to accept help since we're such at ease to give it. There always will be challenging times, but we must maintain our faith, demeanor, unique Southern style, and simply go on.

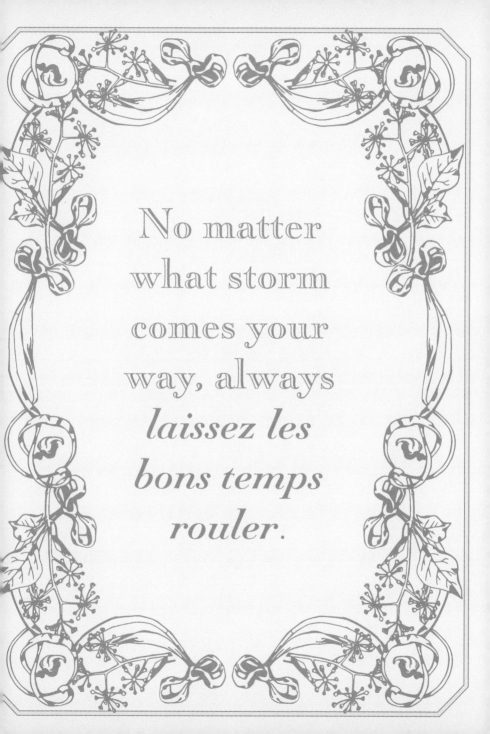

No matter
what storm
comes your
way, always
laissez les
bons temps
rouler.

Well,
I do
declare!

ACCENTS IN THE SOUTH CAN BE AS DIFFERENT AS
the secret seasonings we use in our fried chicken batter. As
soon as we open our mouths, the deep Southern drawl clues
people into exactly what part of the area we're from. But with
so many different dialects, all Southerners speak slowly, our
vowels are usually drawn out, and we often drop the g—we're
fixin', piddlin', listenin', and always eatin'.

Louisiana is probably the most unique area because it has
four dialects: North, Southeast, Southwest, and New Orleans.
People from North Louisiana tend to sound more Texan with
a country twang. Since I moved North, my family and friends
claim I have a "twang" in my accent. With Northerners, you'll
also hear them saying "big o,'" where in other parts of the South
it's "big ole." We also get madder than all git out too! (Learn
more about the other accents in the following pages.)

THE SOUTHEASTERN PART OF LOUISIANA originates from a Cajun background and frequently uses more French words than English—and it shows in their accent. Their words are longer and spoken much slower. If you do not come from a French or Cajun background, you'll need to pay very close attention. The words are so interchangeable from French and English, it can be hard for the average listener to understand what is being said. For example, when it's time to go, someone will tell you, "Allons." When describing the best meat they just ate, they might throw in a "C'est si bon!"—which means it was so good! A favorite around my house, that even my North Louisianan children use, is "envie," something you say when you have a craving. Next time you're asked at work what you'd like for lunch, throw in, "I've got an envie," and enjoy the response!

C'EST SI BON!

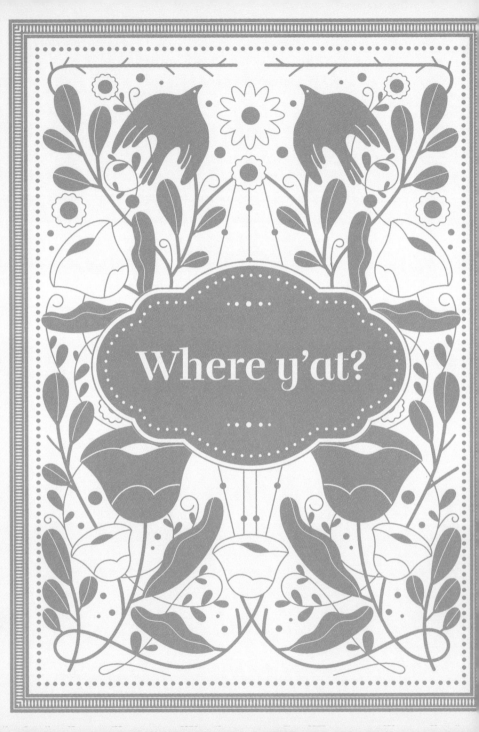

Where y'at?

· · • · ·

IT'S NO SURPRISE THAT NEW ORLEANS HAS A
dialect all its own. Their specific dialect is what people call "Yat."
Yats sound like they are Brooklyn transports, believe it or not.
If you put any true New Orleans resident right up in the mix of
New York City, you'd have a hard time picking out who is who!
The name Yat comes from the New Orleans saying, "Where y'at?"
as in, "Where are you?" They also drop the R in darling, leaving
you with a sharp "daw-lin." New Orleanians also say "doze" for
"those" and rhyme "quarter" and "water."

ARKANSAS, TENNESSEE, AND THE LOWER Appalachian Mountains have what is called a mountain twang. Words that end in -im, -en, or -em end up sounding more like "in." Southeastern Louisiana, Mississippi, Alabama, and Georgia have more of your traditional and well-recognized Southern accent. They are deep, slow, and more melodic—they sound very laid back. Their version of the Southern dialect easily rolls off the tongue, but it is the one most butchered onscreen. Hollywood has decided that everyone that is considered Southern sounds the same, but we know that's not true. We cringe when we hear a terrible fake accent coming from even the most famous of actors. Most people can hear it and not think a thing about it, but us Southerners, we just take a big swig of our cocktail and offer the sweetest "Bless their heart."

Sit down
and rest
yo'self.
Sittin's
cheaper'n
standin'.

MIGHT
COULD

IF YOU USE THE PHRASE "MIGHT COULD," THAT means you might be able to do something, or you are thinking about possibly doing something but without any formal commitment. I might could bring that sweet potato pie to the potluck supper at the church tomorrow, but that doesn't necessarily mean that I will. It's a cute way of making a promise without any intent. If someone ever uses this phrase around you, you might want to call their bluff before you go assuming they mean what they're saying.

How to Plan the Perfect Mardi Gras Party

Mardi Gras is more than just one party. Carnival is the season of parades, festivities, and parties culminating in Mardi Gras, otherwise known as Fat Tuesday. When the day comes, be prepared to throw your own epic party!

• • • •

1. **Send out royalty worthy invitations.** Nothing sets the tone of a party more than the perfect invitation. Adorn your invite with masks, beads, glitter, and of course the mandatory colors of purple, green, and gold! These colors mean more than just a party: purple represents justice, green is for faith, and gold symbolizes power.

2. **Serve a festive menu.** Traditional Cajun fare is the perfect food to serve for a Mardi Gras party. Start things off with grilled shrimp, meat pies, or an andouille and fried gator charcuterie board. Gumbo, jambalaya, and red beans make amazing entrées. Don't forget to top everything off with a traditional king cake.

3. ***Decorate in style.*** Cover your party scene in all things purple, green, and gold. Decorate with bunting and beads and lots of feathered masks, noisemakers, and hats.

4. ***Stock the bar.*** Load up the ice chests with drinks for everyone! Water, soda, beer, and themed cocktails. Hurricanes, mimosas, and Bloody Marys can all be made with or without alcohol for a festive good time!

5. ***Play some tunes.*** Play some festive music like brass band and get everyone dancing. Check your streaming station for themed playlists of Mardi Gras music or New Orleans classics.

· · • · ·

Love
Traditions

outherners simply love love. Maybe it's because we adore throwing around terms of endearment such as "sugar" and "honey," so love is always on our minds. We love warm summer nights and moonlit swims in the lake with a loved one. We may celebrate vegetables and saints with parades, but we celebrate love with huge parties, events, and even bigger weddings.

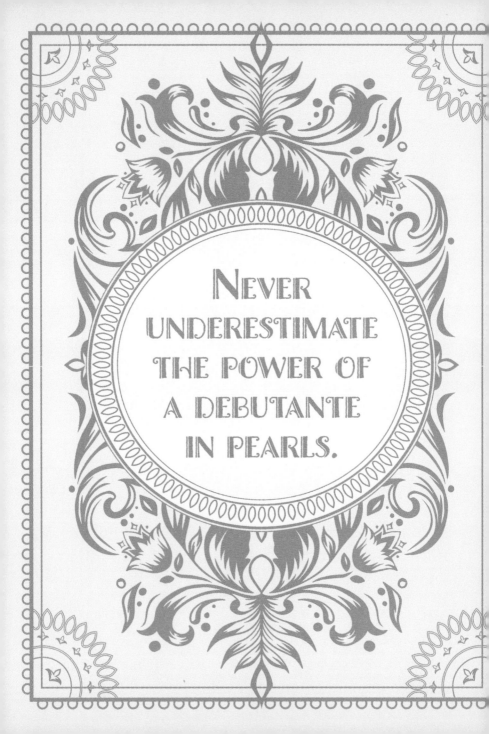

NEVER
UNDERESTIMATE
THE POWER OF
A DEBUTANTE
IN PEARLS.

A DEBUTANTE OR "DEB" BALL CELEBRATES A YOUNG lady's entrance, or "debut," into society in hopes of finding her love. They used to be the way a family announced that their daughter was ready to be married. Debutantes wear formal white gowns, similar to a wedding gown—however, these are never to be re-worn at a wedding. The girls are presented by their father and also by an escort of their choice. The night is filled with dinner, drinks, and, of course, a lot of dancing. Today, while debutante balls do follow certain traditions from the past, the girls presented are usually busy in college. It has become more of a celebration of family, community, and of the deb's achievements.

IF COTILLION IS PREGAME FOR THE DEB BALL, then the wedding is the postseason championship game. (Yes, that is a football reference because football is religion in the South.) Not a lot of weddings happen in the fall because of football season—and also hurricane season, but mainly football! No good Southern bride would dare try to schedule against her home team or the teams of friends and family. The majority of Southern weddings are held outdoors in the spring and summer, prime seersucker-wearing time when most everything is in bloom.

I'D GET GUSSIED UP FOR YOU ANY DAY—EXCEPT IN FALL.

Worth the wait; now it's time to celebrate.

SOUTHERN WEDDINGS ARE USUALLY BIG AND LOUD
and filled with as many traditions as family members. Most
engagements are at least six months long to allow enough
time to fit all the parties in and give the family ample time
to make travel plans if needed. Like deb season, there is the
cocktail announcement party, several themed parties, and the
tea party—and then you also have to add the bachelorette and
bachelor parties, the bridesmaids' luncheon, the rehearsal
dinner, and an after-party . . . and sometimes a going-away
brunch. Just remember, it's a marathon, not a sprint!

SOUTHERN WEDDINGS CONTAIN MANY WELL-KNOWN
traditions, including the four important things on the big day:
something old, new, borrowed, and blue. In my wedding I had
a sixpence in my shoe (old), my dress (new), a pair of diamond
studs from my grandmother, Big Girl Aud (borrowed), and
a handkerchief with my wedding date and the dates of my
mother and grandmothers' weddings embroidered on it (blue).
If you've ever shopped at Southern boutiques, they often sell
cards with lucky sixpence coins, and dainty handkerchiefs just
waiting for embroidery.

IF THE DRESS
AIN'T NEW,
SOMETHING ELSE'S
GOTTA BE.

Let's bury
a bottle
of bourbon
just in case
it's thinking
of raining.

IF YOU WANT TO ENSURE BEAUTIFUL WEATHER ON your wedding day, there is one very Southern way to make it happen. Exactly one month before the wedding, at the exact time of the ceremony, the bride and groom should bury a bottle of bourbon at the site of the wedding. There are some specific rules as to how it should be done. The bottle of bourbon should be full and unopened, and it should be buried upside down. It must also be real bourbon and not whiskey. Real bourbon is made of 51 percent corn mash, made in the United States, and aged in an oak-charred barrel. It must be no less than 80 proof. After the wedding, the groom digs up the bottle, he and his new wife take the first drink, and then they share it with their wedding party and whoever else wishes to imbibe with them.

THE SECOND LINE STARTED IN NEW ORLEANS BUT
made its way all across the South. After the wedding, the bride
and groom lead the way to the reception hall. They usually
carry white parasols, sometimes decorated with flowers or
streamers. A brass band (the first line) accompanies them
with all the guests following behind waving handkerchiefs
(the second line). It's not uncommon to see a second line in the
French Quarter. As long as you don't crash the reception as an
uninvited guest, most observers are more than welcome to join
in the parade and celebrate the new bride and groom. Second
lines, or bridal parades, also can be found in Mexico.

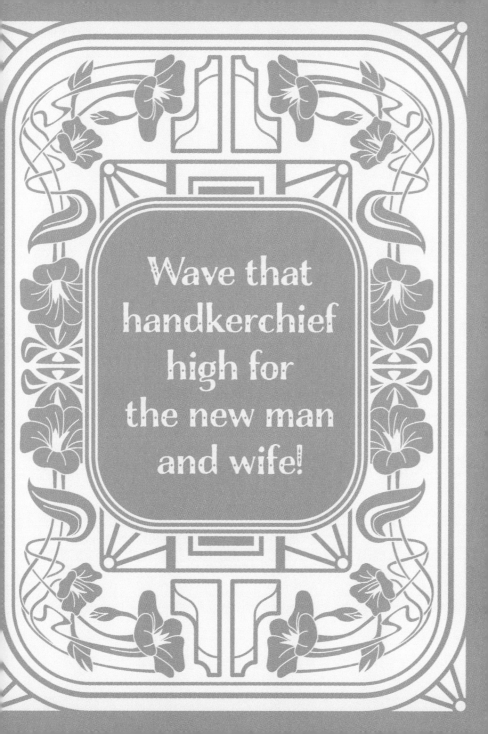

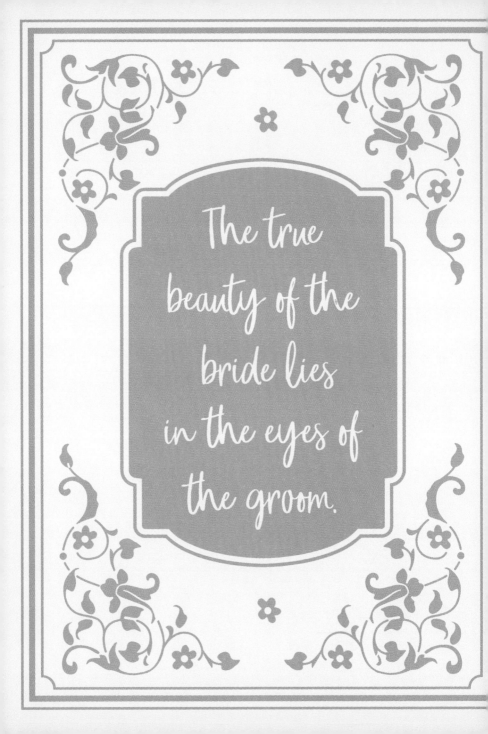

The true beauty of the bride lies in the eyes of the groom.

SOUTHERN BRIDES ARE KNOWN TO DO A DAY of run-throughs, which means trying on the full wedding makeup, their hairstyle, and the dress to make sure they look the perfect Southern bride for their groom. And if you're going to go to all that trouble, you might as well document it. Brides will book their wedding photographer to take their picture either at the wedding venue or the bride's home before the big day. The portrait is framed and displayed at the wedding, usually at the entrance to the reception by the guest book. (We all know the wedding is really about the bride anyway.)

CAKE PULLS ARE A FUN FORTUNE-TELLING TRADITION just for the bridesmaids. Metal charms are tied to ribbons and carefully placed between the layers of the wedding cake. Right before the bride and groom cut the cake, the bride gathers with her bridesmaids so they can pull a charm. Each bridesmaid chooses a ribbon, and at the same time, they pull the charms out of the cake. The charm attached is believed to reveal the fate for each bridesmaid.

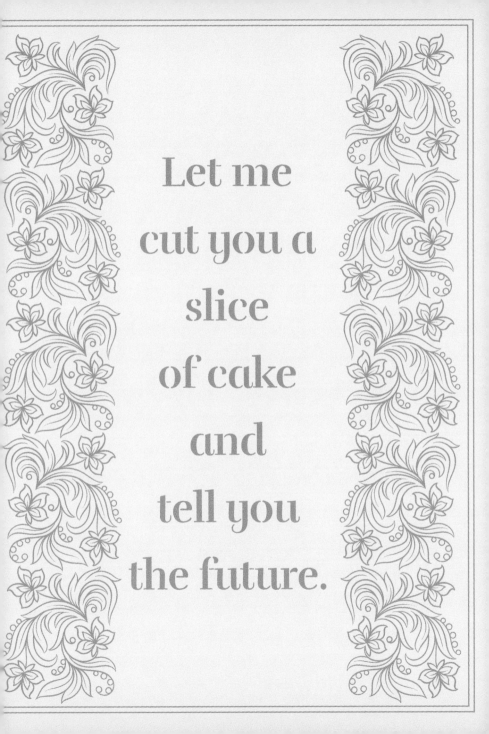

Let me
cut you a
slice
of cake
and
tell you
the future.

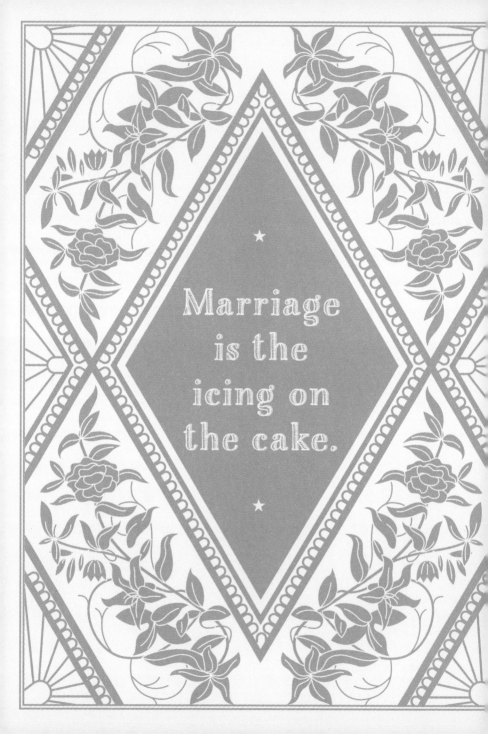

Marriage
is the
icing on
the cake.

THE GROOM'S CAKE IS A GIFT FROM THE BRIDE TO THE groom. Sometimes the cake's theme is a surprise to the groom, and sometimes he is included in the planning. If it's a surprise, the bride presents the cake to him after their arrival at the wedding reception. The cake represents the groom's hobbies, career, or maybe a funny joke between the couple. It is also more adventurous in flavors and décor. My husband's cake was a scale model of the LSU football stadium with the mascot, Mike the Tiger, climbing over the sidewall. The cake was chocolate with chocolate chip ganache filling and was 3 feet (0.9 m) long by 2 feet (0.6 m) wide. His cake was a surprise and he loved it. Geaux Tigers!

THE POUNDING PARTY TAKES PLACE AFTER THE honeymoon. Friends and family gather one last time to welcome home the newly married couple. They stock their pantry with food staples by the pound. For example, they gift flour, sugar, eggs, butter, and so on. It's also a time to look at wedding pictures if they are ready to reminisce about the good time had by all.

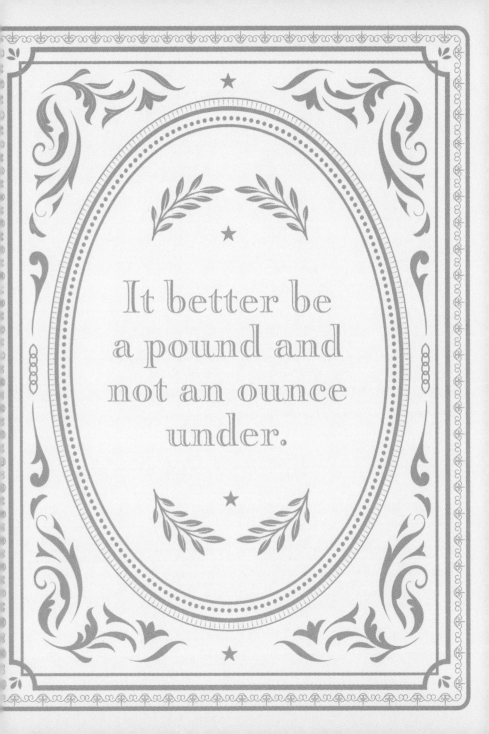

It better be
a pound and
not an ounce
under.

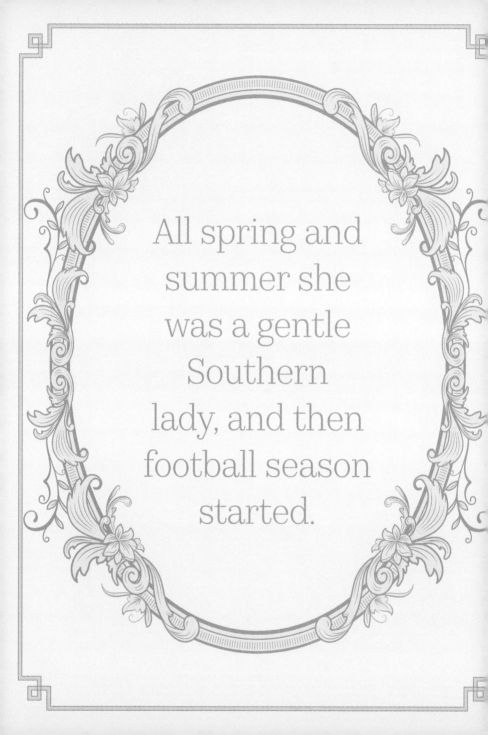

All spring and
summer she
was a gentle
Southern
lady, and then
football season
started.

FOOTBALL, BELIEVE IT OR NOT, CAN HELP IN matchmaking. In the South it's a tradition for a young college man to ask for a date to a game. In the Greek system, most fraternities require their pledges to bring a date. The guys are dressed in their sharp blue blazers with freshly pressed khakis, and the girls go in their colorful game day best. However, just as many relationships have ended as have started at a football game. Tailgates can get rowdy and proper behavior can slip by the wayside after a few whiskey drinks. God forbid, the team of choice loses . . . Let's just say, the ladies are known to throw hissy fits that rival the guys.

WHEN WE SAY WE DON'T DISCUSS RELIGION, THAT can apply to football too. They say opposites attract and there is no greater example of that than college football fans. There are just as many homes divided by football in the South as there are that support the same team. Perhaps they met at a tailgate party or even at a bar after the game. Large families don't always end up at the same school, but those rivalries are just as much fun off the field as they are on the field. Sometimes, states can even be divided! In Northern Louisiana, we tend to support the Dallas Cowboys due to close proximity instead of the Saints who are right down in New Orleans. No matter who you root for though, we share a common love for the game. Football, for us Southerners, is just another form of community, love, and a way to make new friends.

OUR HOME
MAY BE DIVIDED,
BUT OUR
HEARTS ARE
UNITED.

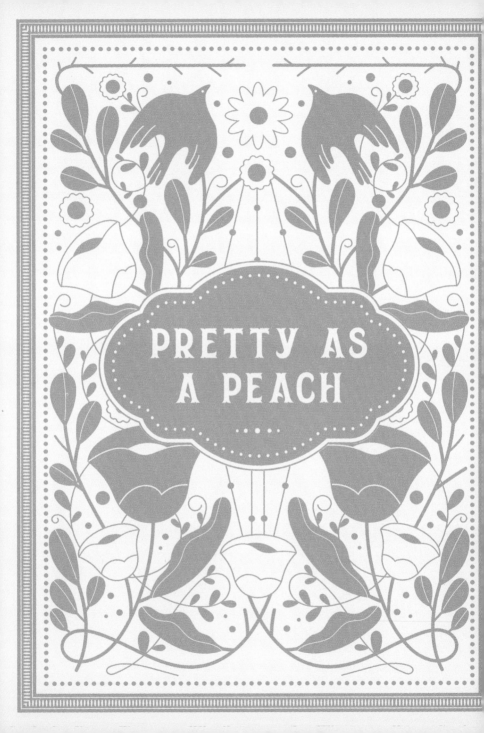

PRETTY AS
A PEACH

• • ● • •

PEACHES ARE AN IMPORTANT FRUIT IN THE SOUTH.
Set foot anywhere in the state of Georgia and it's easy to
get lost in the large amount of Peach Tree Streets, Avenues,
Boulevards, and Circles. It's the state's fruit, so peaches grace
the names of businesses, parades, and countless events too.
When someone says you're as pretty as a peach, you can take
that as one of the highest compliments.

• • ● • •

Cake Pull Charms and Their Meanings

Going back to the tradition of cake pulls at a wedding, here is a list of some of the charms that might be attached to a ribbon and what it means for the bridesmaid who pulls it. Remember, if you use this tradition at your own wedding, designate appropriate charms for single and married bridesmaids to make it a little more realistic. Different colored ribbons or a simple ink dot on the end will help you differentiate which is which.

· · ● · ·

1. **Airplane:** Exotic travel adventures are in your near future.

2. **Highchair:** You will be blessed with children.

3. **Owl:** You are full of wisdom.

4. **Rocker:** You will be blessed with a long life.

5. **Heart:** You will be lucky in love.

6. **Horseshoe or four-leaf clover:** You will have good luck.

7. **Telephone:** Good news is coming.

8. **Anchor:** Hope is coming.

9. **Ring:** You will be the next to get married.

10. **Dice:** May good fortune find you.

11. **Butterfly:** You will have eternal beauty.

12. **Fleur-de-lis:** May your greatest devotion be to yourself.

13. **Oyster:** May prosperity join you.

· · · · ·

Ain't We Charming?

★ ★ ★ ★ ★

In the South, there are no strangers, just friends we have not yet met. One area where Southerners simply shine is in our charm and hospitality. The stereotype that all Southerners are warm and welcoming is welcomed; however, don't let that fool you into believing we are always charming. Southerners also can be the biggest gossips you've ever met. We have the power to insult you to your face, yet you will still be thanking us for it. It all comes back to that charm.

★ ★ ★ ★ ★

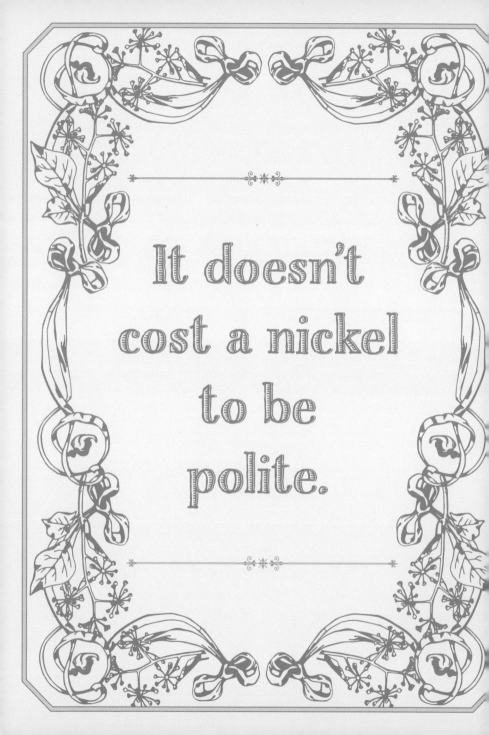

It doesn't cost a nickel to be polite.

THERE ARE MANY THINGS THAT MAKE UP SOUTHERN charm. First is the art of manners. It doesn't cost you anything to have them. It is something you're taught. Hold the door open for those behind you and do it with a smile. Be sure to always wave at your neighbor, and if short on time, give the two-finger salute when behind the steering wheel. When you can devote adequate time, the best example of manners is proper conversation. Nothing puts people more at ease than not having to struggle with conversation or make awkward small talk. The simplest way Southerners start a conversation is to ask easy questions about your family and where you're from. This can oh so quickly lead into investigating your own personal history, and before you know it, you're sharing your grandma's recipe for her sweet potato casserole and being invited to Thanksgiving dinner!

TO CLOSE OFF ANY GOSSIP-FILLED CONVERSATION, always throw in a "Bless your heart" to make sure you're showing equal part condescension and sweetness. It also can be used when there just isn't anything you can say or do to make something better. If a man goes out with a woman and finds she's just a little bit crazy, "Bless his heart." If a daughter did something that is sure to get back to her mother, "Bless her heart." If you don't order grits while you're visiting the South, "Bless your heart."

Bless
your
heart.

YOU
GOTTA
GET
GUSSIED UP!

GETTING DRESSED UP IS A FAVORITE PASTIME
for us, whether it's going to church or even to the local grocery.
Any good Southern grandmother will tell you, "You never know
who you will run into, so you best be in your best when you go
out." Just as important is to not forget the monogram. Putting
our initials on our things is of the highest importance.

Just like we had uniforms in school, we had them out of
school as well. Little Southern girls wear smock dresses, white
ruffled socks with matching patent leather shoes, and, of
course, we cannot forget the hairbow. The younger gentleman
wears what is lovingly referred to as the frat boy uniform:
khaki pants, white-buttoned down shirt, navy blue sports
blazer, and either a tie or bow tie with bucks or deck shoes. Of
course, there is a monogram on their shirt, cuff links, tiepin,
or even socks.

SOUTHERN CHILDREN ARE TAUGHT FROM DAY ONE
how to engage in conversation. I learned from an early age how
to converse with an adult when addressed. Now, I might not
have always followed those rules, but I sure did know them.
When a child is spoken to, they should enunciate their words,
look someone straight in the eye, and speak up—no one likes a
mumbler. When starting a conversation, the best way to begin
is a firm handshake. Handshakes are the globally accepted
form of greeting, and Southerners are masters of them. Firmly
reach out with a straight wrist and give them your full hand.
Always match their amount of squeeze and give a nice smile.
A handshake tells a lot about a person and it's the best way to
give a good first impression.

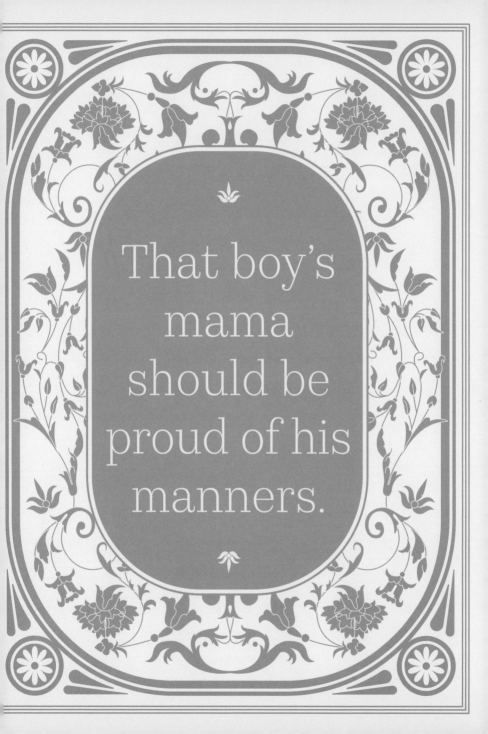

That boy's mama should be proud of his manners.

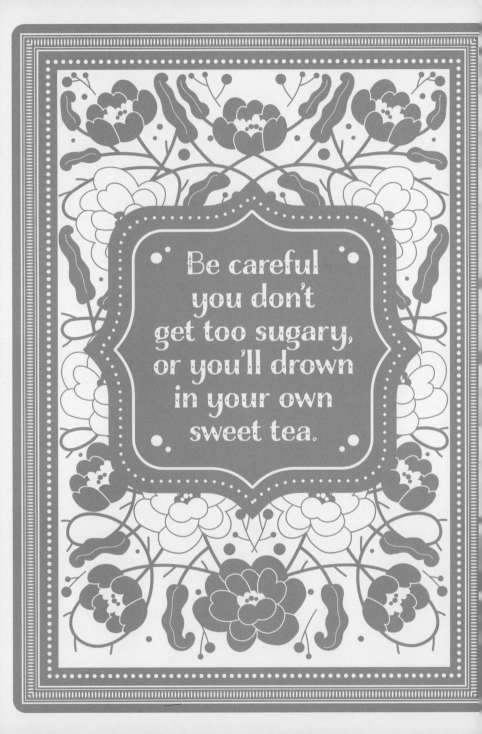

WE HAVE A LOVE OF CREATIVE WORDS, NICKNAMES, and terms of endearment. Giving compliments in the South is pretty easy; just use your most creative and descriptive words, throw in a fruit or vegetable reference or two, and say it really slowly. We love a sweet pea, a sugar pie, or even a dumplin'. If you throw in a "pretty as a" before any of those words, well you might have just crowned the next Ms. USA!

But beware, we love to disguise our insults as compliments. If you're not originally from the South and you didn't grow up with grandmothers or aunts telling you, in the sweetest of ways, your dress doesn't match your jewelry or your hair is all a mess, what is said to you could be a little hard to decipher. Just remember, if it sounds too sweet, it's probably an insult.

IN THE EIGHTEENTH-CENTURY, THE WORD *COTILLION* was used to describe a group dance by the French and the English. This was the precedent of the square dance. Cotillion is a social club where Southern children learn the rules of etiquette and valuable social skills such as proper social graces and how to be confident and converse confidently. Cotillion classes meet weekly and Southern children learn how to dance the waltz or the foxtrot while dressed in their Sunday best. Once you get to high school, you attend larger quarterly parties where you're able to bring a date, have fun, and put those social graces to use. These parties usually are held at a prestigious hall or the local country club and feature a prominent regional band—getting to go was quite the treasured invite as a teenager.

Teach them how to dance and they'll learn some manners.

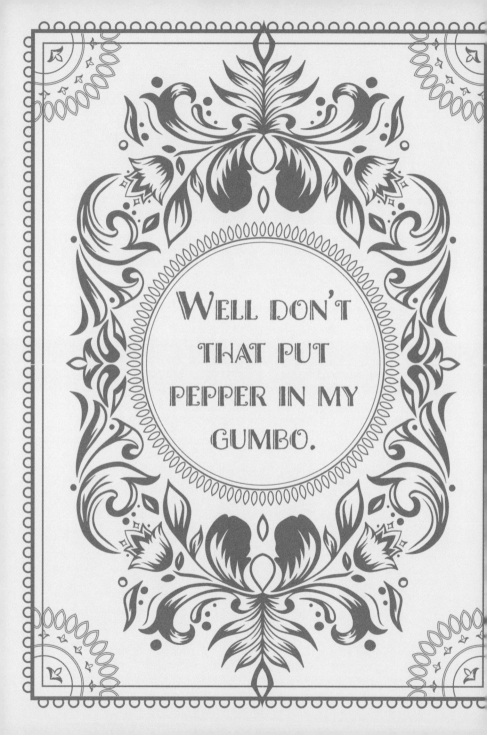

WELL DON'T THAT PUT PEPPER IN MY GUMBO.

ANOTHER WAY SOUTHERNERS EASILY ENGAGE IN conversation is through gossip. Given all our creative expressions, we camouflage talking about one another with a myriad of words that sound sweet but are actually not. We can talk about someone who won't admit to their wrongdoing by saying, "It's always the dirty dog that howls the loudest." Or suppose you're talking about someone who is just not friendly. "She's as cold as a cast-iron toilet seat." This phrase conjures up vivid imagery that will surely make you understand the seriousness of her behavior!

OUR FAVORITE PEOPLE TO GOSSIP ABOUT HAVE got to be our neighbors. While we are a culture that thrives on community, if a neighbor does one bad thing, bless their hearts, they're going straight to the top of every gossip list. "He's always looking for sundown and a payday" might be the most common thing someone would say about a neighbor they dislike. It means he's lazy and worthless. Maybe he doesn't mow his lawn until it gets unruly. Or he didn't put out his trash can on time, and you had to do it for him. Or you saw him outside once in ratty pajamas and haven't let it go since. While a Southerner will be cordial and polite to your face, if you're their neighbor, they're probably complaining about you.

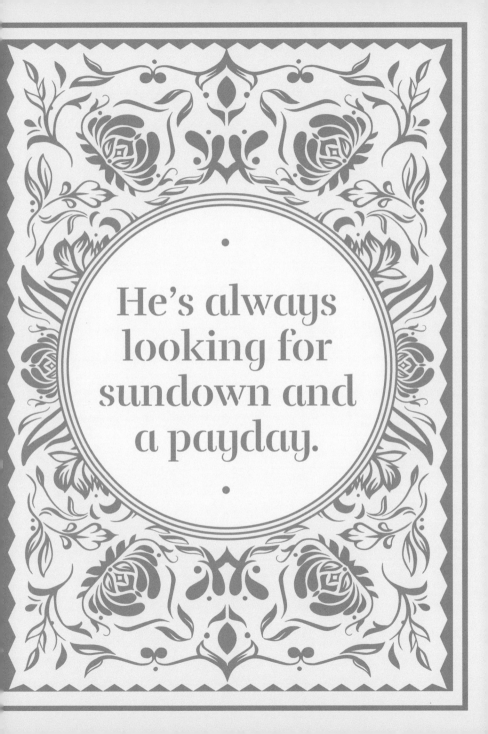

He's always looking for sundown and a payday.

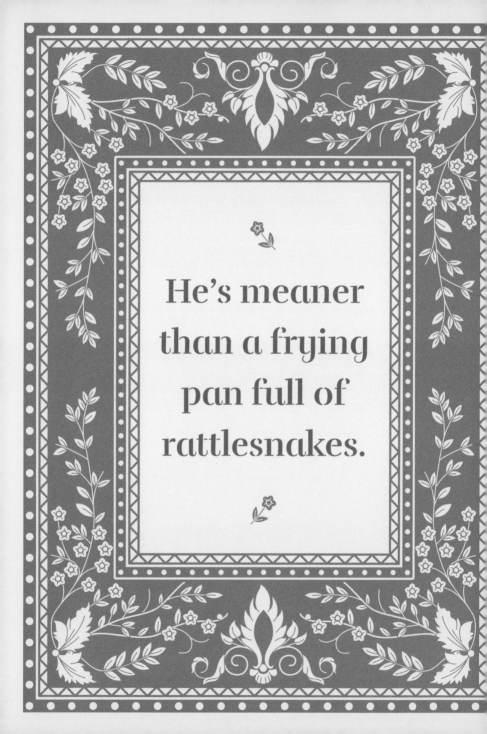

He's meaner than a frying pan full of rattlesnakes.

HE'S MEAN, MEAN, AND JUST MEAN FOR SPORT. THIS
saying is a combination of two staple items in the South.
Everyone who lives here should have a good frying pan. And
not just a decent one, but their favorite one that they use for
gatherings and special occasions because it's just that good.
The hot weather and swamps also make it home to snakes,
specifically rattlesnakes. They sometimes take up residence
under our front porches, and if you ever see one, you should go
the other way because they are mean and poisonous.

THERE IS SUCH A THING AS BEING TOO POLITE TO the point that it goes to your head. This saying means, "She's so spoiled even the good Lord couldn't help her!" While we like to be well dressed and say our ma'ams and sirs and have a blessed day, Southerners don't like that high-and-mighty personality that is sometimes associated with pageant queens. If you can't get your boots muddied up, or lend a helping hand, or smile and wave when passing someone by, then no one's going to try to fix you. But we sure will gossip about ya!

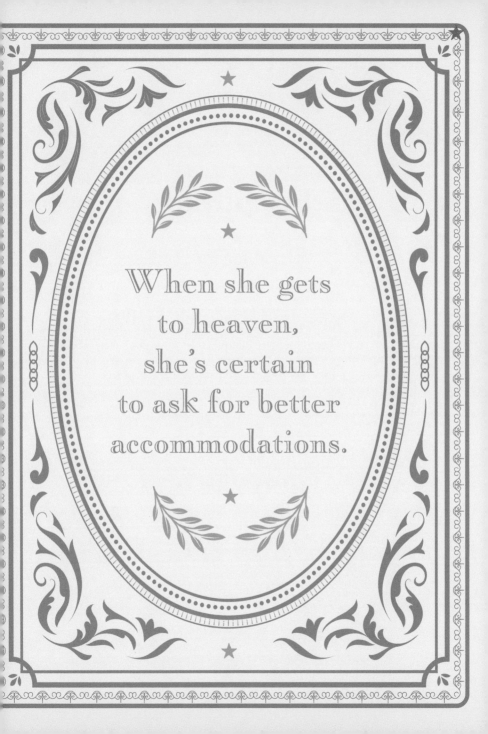

When she gets
to heaven,
she's certain
to ask for better
accommodations.

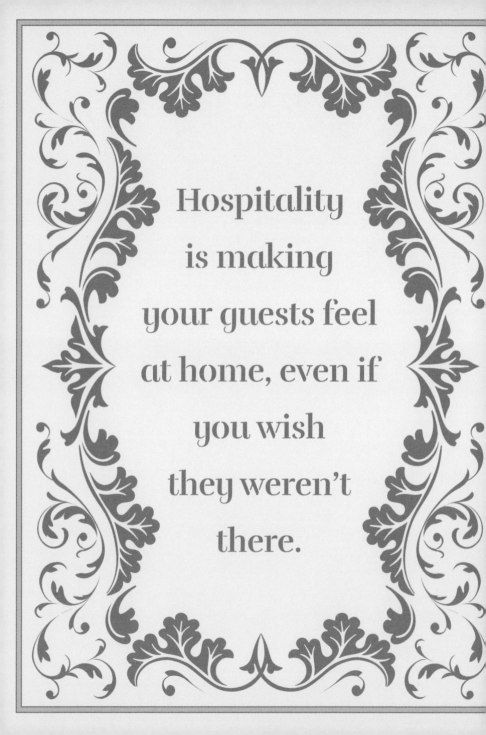

Hospitality
is making
your guests feel
at home, even if
you wish
they weren't
there.

WHEN YOU ARE BLESSED WITH HUGE FAMILIES, BEING A good hostess is something you develop over time. I grew up watching my mother, grandmothers, and a multitude of aunts and friends play host to huge parties and family gatherings. They organized Christmas dinners, wedding and baby showers, and funeral receptions with the skill and planning of an army general going into battle. Tables are set days in advance with little cards or sticky notes indicating what will be placed where (nothing is left to chance). Pantries and refrigerators are stocked with essentials such as serving platters, cloth napkins, extra wine, crackers, and cheese, all to be used at a moment's notice. Care and extreme attention to detail goes into every event, because for Southern women this is a form of showing respect and our good manners.

COMFORT IS KEY IN THE SOUTH, AND WE LOVE TO dress for it. While we may love our dress attire, the favored outfit in the South is none other than a good pair of blue jeans, a comfortable shirt, and nice leather cowboy boots. Ladies don't just wear boots with jeans—we love them best with a sundress and so do our fellas. The men love to wear a white T-shirt in the spring and summer or a nice long-sleeve flannel in the fall. Cowboy boots only get better with age, so when you decide to make the investment, buy what's comfortable, buy a style that matches you most, and buy real leather. The heat plays a major factor in fashion and dictates how people dress. Seersucker fabric was invented for this reason. This striped, puckered cotton fabric never lays flat on the skin, so it keeps you cool as you go from day to night.

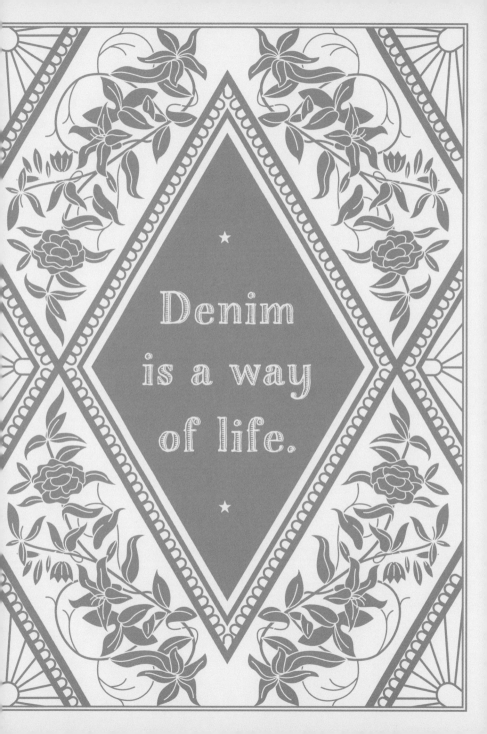

Denim
is a way
of life.

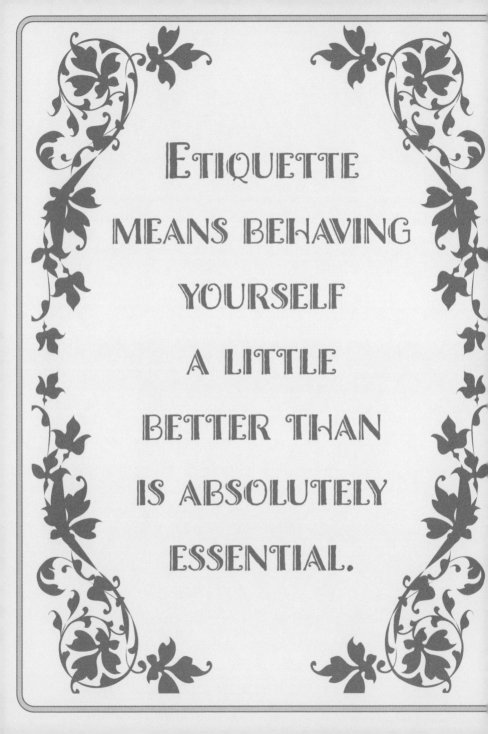

ETIQUETTE
MEANS BEHAVING
YOURSELF
A LITTLE
BETTER THAN
IS ABSOLUTELY
ESSENTIAL.

SOUTHERN CHILDREN, BOTH GIRLS AND BOYS, ARE taught the importance of learning to write the perfect thank-you note from the get-go. Not only are we perfecting our manners, but we're also improving our handwriting, as thank-you notes should always be handwritten. I've had personalized stationery all my life—the only thing that has changed is my monogram. Thank-you notes are given after every birthday, religious ceremony, and basically anytime you receive a gift. Pay attention to the details of the gift and be specific in your note about how it will be used. This tradition should extend into our careers, to be given after interviews and other business opportunities. But this whole exercise in handwriting and manners, however, is really to work us up for when we will write the most thank-you notes . . . after the wedding!

The Perfect Southern Thank-You Note

As we get older, the importance of a thank-you note grows. Writing a thank-you note is a thoughtful and personal gesture to show your gratitude for a gift or action, like being invited to a lovely dinner party. Sending a thank-you note to the person who interviewed you for a job also could be what sets you apart and lands you the job. Here are some important tips to writing the perfect Southern thank-you note.

• • • • •

1. **Buy REAL stationery.** While it's nice, you do not need to invest in embossed, personalized stationery. Simple thank you note cards with matching envelopes from your local stationery store will do.

2. **Handwrite, don't type.** Email or text may be the preferred method of communication today, but taking the time to write the note yourself, in ink, shows how important it is to you.

3. **Personalize it.** Think before you write. Think about what was given to you and for what occasion. Tell the recipient

how much you appreciate it, and if it's a physical gift, where you might use it in your home. However, don't overdo it. They will know if you're exaggerating by saying it's the absolute best gift you've ever received in your entire life. Be truthful, thoughtful, and grateful.

4. ***Avoid specific amounts of money.*** Southerners might not ever like to discuss money, but if it's given to you, you must say thanks for it. Do not say thank you for the specific dollar amount but say thanks for the generosity. You may include your plans for the money, as long as you think the recipient would approve.

• • ● • •

Food
Talk

Food is just as important as location or religion in the South—maybe even more so. If you ever plan on visiting, make sure you're prepared to eat a lot. Comfort meals are our signature, so save room in your stomachs, and while you're at it, learn a few of our sayings that relate to food.

Good
food
brings
families
together.

IF THE SOUTH IS KNOWN FOR ANYTHING, IT'S writing things down and passing them on through the generations. However, sharing meals and recipes is not just a Southern thing. A recipe card can bring back a treasured family memory so fast you can almost smell it. Like the genealogy binders, these recipes are handwritten cards. I personally have a binder full of my grandmothers' and aunts' beautiful handwriting that I will treasure forever. Junior Leagues across the South compile cookbooks of recipes credited to women that serve as a fundraiser for their community activities. It is considered an honor to have your recipe included. You'll also notice the chef of your family standing up a little straighter if their recipe is picked.

THAT SAYING IS THE START OF MANY A GREAT recipe handed down. A roux is an important staple in the Southern kitchen. It's a cooked mixture of equal parts flour and fat used to thicken sauces and stews. Fats can range from butter, oil, lard, or drippings from bacon or other meats. Mastering a roux takes time, practice, and patience. Burning it is a horrible, stinky experience no one wants to have because you'll never forget the smell and you certainly will not admit to ever having done it. If you ever enter a kitchen in the South and someone says these famous first words, and you've never made a roux before, bless your heart.

but first
you make
a roux…

THE BEST
THINGS COME
TO THOSE WHO
WAIT.

WHILE GRANDMOTHERS ARE THE BACKBONE OF the Southern family, grits are the backbone of the Southern kitchen. Grits can be stone-ground, yellow, and white. Stone-ground grits are dried corn kernels that have been coarsely ground in a grist mill. Using this old-fashioned method, they often have a speckled appearance, a thicker texture, and a deeper flavor, which makes them the favorite in Southern kitchens.

The best things come to those who wait, and this applies to grits as well. Real grits take some time to cook, so be patient. A real Southerner would never even entertain the idea of using instant grits! You can find grits served with butter and salt at any roadside dive or topped with the freshest seafood from the Gulf or the juiciest grilled meats at the fanciest restaurants in the South.

WHEN IT COMES TO BBQ, THERE ARE MANY KINDS that designate what part of the South you're in. While Elvis was king of the music scene, pork and specifically pork ribs ruled over the Memphis BBQ kingdom. It could be wet style: brushing the meat with a thin sauce by pitmasters before, during, and after smoking the meat of choice. Or dry style: meat coated in a dry spice rub and then smoked without any sauce.

In Texas, the Holy Trinity is ribs, sausage links, and, best of all, brisket. Pitmasters can smoke a brisket for up to eighteen hours. They rub it with dry spices, and their BBQ sauce is usually made from meat drippings and mixed with Worcestershire and hot sauce.

We have Memphis-made Henry Perry to thank for bringing Kansas City his style of BBQ. His specific style is used on a variety of meat, while the BBQ sauce is thick and sugary made from brown sugar, molasses, and tomatoes.

But it's the Carolina style of BBQ that is the oldest style of cooking meat in America. They smoke the whole hog for twelve to twenty-four hours and use a mop sauce made from vinegar, apple cider, tomato juice, and sometimes beer!

THE HIGH SOCIETY OF BBQ

Pinch, peel, eat, repeat

NOTHING SAYS SPRINGTIME IN THE SOUTH MORE than a newspaper-covered table of piping hot crawfish! Crawfish boils stretch from Texas all the way to Georgia and each area puts its own spin and ingredients in the pot! Crawfish go by many names: mudbugs, crayfish, crawdads, but they all taste the same.

Crawfish boils date way back to the swamps of western Louisiana and the Cajuns. Each spring, the floodwaters force the crawfish to leave their burrows where the Cajuns await. Crawfish season falls during Lent—the time after Ash Wednesday but before Easter—usually from March to April.

Each crawfish pot is filled to the brim with "the fixins": corn, potatoes, andouille sausage, shrimp, alligator bits, green beans, asparagus, mushrooms, lemons, artichokes, and garlic. Crawfish boils are so highly thought of in the South that Louisiana annually pardons one crawfish each year just like the president pardons a turkey at Thanksgiving.

WE CAN'T DISCUSS FOOD OF THE SOUTH WITHOUT talking about drinking alcohol. With alcohol present at almost every social gathering, there is sure to be someone who overdoes it. Cooter Brown lived in a small Cajun shack along the Mason-Dixon Line. When the Civil War began, he had family on both sides and didn't know which side to choose. He figured if he stayed drunk, he wouldn't have to choose and neither side would enlist him. Somehow it worked, and he ended up a drinking man's hero.

He was drunker than Cooter Brown.

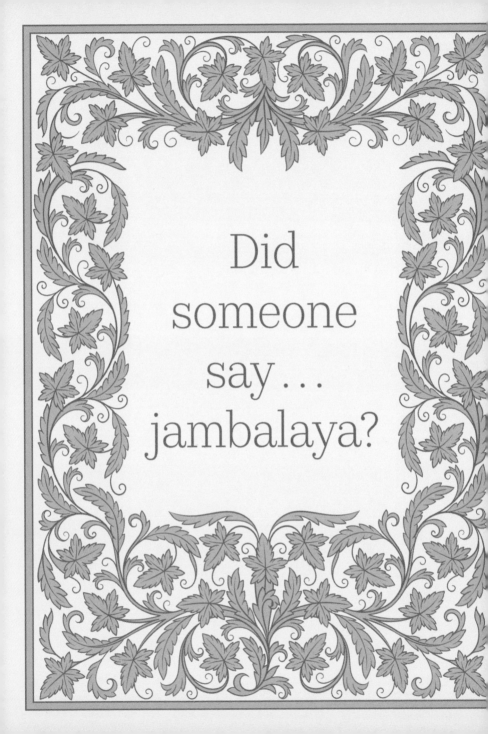

Did someone say … jambalaya?

JAMBALAYA IS A SOUTHERN STAPLE. IT'S A COMFORT food that just makes the belly happy. It's warm and spicy at the same time. Jambalaya is mostly known as a Louisiana rice dish originating from African and European cuisine and based on Spanish paella. My husband is famous for his jambalaya. The recipe is actually a family recipe from my uncle that my husband has made his own. He cooks jambalaya for our annual Mardi Gras party, feeding anywhere between seventy-five to one hundred people.

AT THIS POINT YOU'RE PROBABLY THINKING, "Wow, Southerners can eat." You even might have had to loosen your pants just thinking about all the good food you'll be having soon. When it comes to dessert, it holds a special place at the table—a really large table! Every recipe card in the box uses real sugar; don't use that fake stuff! The sweeter the better, we say. Dessert can be comfort food too, a way to bring people together over a sweet dish and extend the conversation and the good times. Many of my childhood memories, especially with my grandparents, have a special dessert attached to them. My most prominent is my grandmother, Big Girl Aud, and her famous bourbon balls, traditionally made at Christmas. We always say that they are so good, we should make them year-round!

GIMME
SOME SUGAR.

RAISED
BY SWEET
TEA AND
SUNSHINE

IN THE SOUTH, THE SUMMER DAYS CAN EASILY
reach over 100 degrees Fahrenheit (38°C). I have fond
memories of my mother setting out a big glass container
with yellow trim to make sun tea. Instead of heating up your
kitchen by boiling water on a warm summer day, we brew our
tea outside in the sun because it's hot enough to do so. Just fill
your glass container with water and eight tea bags and set it
in direct sunlight for three to five hours. Sun tea doesn't keep
as long in the fridge as tea made with boiling water. It only
lasts about two days, but during the summer, it shouldn't be a
problem to drink it all up in time!

IN THE BATTLE OF SODA VS. POP VS. COKE, COKE REIGNS supreme in the South when discussing soft drinks. Coke (a shortened version for Coca-Cola) is not just used for that brand but for any soft drink you may be craving. The Coca-Cola brand was founded in Atlanta, Georgia, by local pharmacist John Pemberton in 1886. Southerners are always loyal to their own, so maybe that's why we stick with calling everything a Coke. Next time you're in a Southern restaurant, don't be shocked when you order a Coke and the waitress proceeds to ask what kind you want.

Can I get a Coke?

THREE
SHEETS
TO THE
WIND

THE 1800S WERE HEADY DAYS FOR DRINKING in all the United States, but especially in the South. Storytelling and drinking go hand in hand with three sheets of paper flying in the wind symbolizing a person who has drank so much that a soft wind could blow them over.

AMERICA'S ONLY ORIGINAL SPIRIT WAS CREATED in the South. Made from Kentucky corn, bourbon hasn't changed much since the Bottled in Bond Act of 1897. This act set the standards for spirits to be officially labeled as bourbon: The liquor must be made in the United States, must be at least 51 percent corn mash, and must be aged in charred oak barrels. Bourbon is the main ingredient in the old-fashioned cocktail—a true favorite in the South, especially in my family.

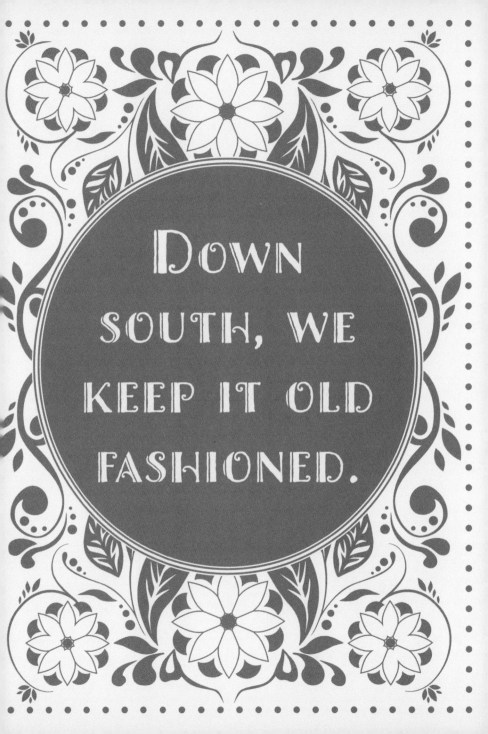

It's gumbo weather!

WHEN THE FIRST COOL BREEZE HITS THE South, we say one thing immediately . . . it's gumbo weather! There are two types of gumbo: chicken and sausage or seafood. And when I say seafood, I mean *all* the seafood: shrimp, fish, alligator, crawfish, crab, and even some sausage thrown in too for extra flavor. Gumbo comes from West Africa and the word *ki ngombo*, meaning okra, which was used as a thickener. The Native Americans contributed sassafras to gumbo and the Europeans introduced the roux base. Today, it's got a long history, and you don't want to miss out on the delicious final result.

THIS CLASSIC BOURBON AND MINT COCKTAIL IS most closely identified as the cocktail of choice at the Kentucky Derby. Kentucky is famous for two things, bourbon and horse racing, and they go hand in hand. The mint julep is served in silver cups to mimic the silver trophies given to the winner of the race. On average, nearly 120,000 mint juleps will be served at Churchill Downs on Derby weekend! That means more than 10,000 bottles of bourbon, 1,000 pounds (453.6 kg) of mint leaves, and 60,000 pounds (2721.6 kg) of ice will be used during this famous horse race. There is even a National Mint Julep Day on May 30 to celebrate this Southern staple.

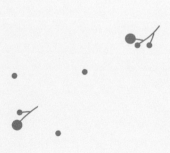

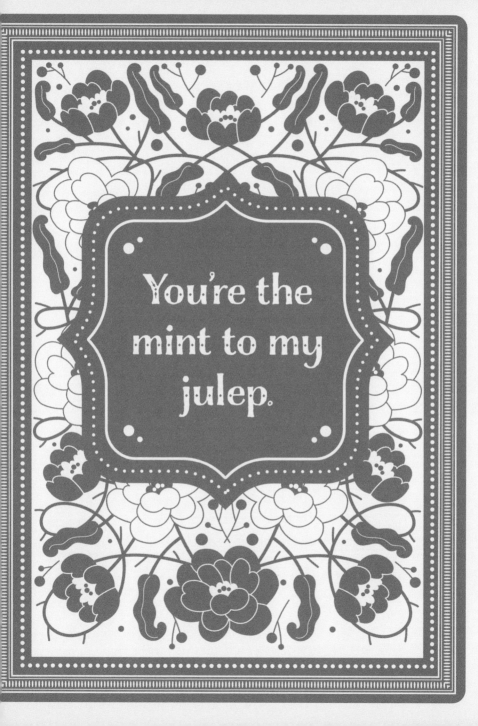

You're the mint to my julep.

Tips for Hosting

A proper Southern hostess exhibits grace and style effortlessly, and if needed, they can change it up at a moment's notice. The goal is to make people feel at ease and welcome no matter the situation. Here are ten tried-and-true hostess tips to make your next get-together flow seamlessly and effortlessly.

• • ● ● •

1. *Welcome your guests.* Always start with a smile and a warm greeting.

2. *Next, offer them a drink.* A Southern hostess always has a stocked bar of not just alcohol, but also a pitcher of ice-cold sweet tea, lemonade, or even bottles of sparkling water with a tray of fresh fruit for flavor.

3. *Fill your guests' tummies.* No one wants a grumpy guest, so make sure to offer some light hors d'oeuvres that are tasty but not too filling.

4. *Serve food that tastes good.* In other words, the food does not have to be gourmet. Whether you are serving a sit-down meal or buffet, a meal of delicious food shows you care.

5. *Music can make or break a party.* One effortless way to get conversations started is with a great playlist. Make sure the

volume is not too loud, so your guests don't have to scream to be heard.

6. ***Let guests help!*** Chances are you'll have other hostesses at your party who know the stress that comes with throwing a party. When a guest offers to help, let them! You can also start educating the next generation of mini hosts and hostesses by letting the kids fold napkins or set the table.

7. ***Set the table with cloth table linens.*** Use fresh flowers, garden clippings, and shop from your home. If you can, break out your china, silver, and crystal. What is the point of having it if you don't use it?

8. ***End the meal with something sweet.*** While I do love to entertain and cook, for me, baking is not my forte. Luckily, my daughter excels at it, so I always leave the dessert to her.

9. ***Outsource where you can.*** Throwing a party and making a meal can be a big undertaking and there is no shame in picking up a cake at the best bakery in town or getting your centerpiece from a local florist.

10. ***Make your guests feel special.*** Make sure you take a moment to chat with each one of your guests and tell them how happy you are they could join you. Simple gestures make all the difference, and a true Southern hostess lets everyone know they are loved and included.

Plenty Superstitious

Southerners love our superstitions. We simply do and it's not something we're ashamed of. I come from a very superstitious family—a fact that drives my husband crazy. We don't think of it as weird or crazy; we file it with our version of Southern charm. Some of these superstitions come from religion, some from family tradition, and some from all the great explorers who landed in the South from Texas to South Carolina. While these may seem silly to some, they are history and traditions passed down and family memories to be respected.

As long as it's got a haint blue ceiling, you'll be safe.

THE HAINT BLUE COLOR WAS USED TO PAINT THE ceilings of front porches in the South to deter spiders, wasps, and other insects from building nests and webs and interrupting leisurely porch sitting. The blue color was thought to fool the insects into thinking that the ceiling was the sky. A pale-blue paint color also was thought to prevent evil spirits, a superstition that goes back to the Gullah Geechee, the enslaved people in the eastern Southern states. They believed that ghosts, or "haints," could not cross water. Haint blue is also not one specific color of blue. It is rather a range of colors to emulate the blue sky. Your specific shade of blue should work with the style of your house.

AN ITCHY NOSE IS OFTEN THOUGHT TO BE A SIGN that an unexpected visitor is on their way to see you. The visitor could be someone you know or perhaps a stranger who has the ability to change your life for the better or worse. If your nose itches on the left side, it means you'll receive a male visitor. If it itches on the right side, a female visitor is coming. So, like mama always says, get gussied up as you never know who you're going to meet.

Get ready,
my nose
itches.

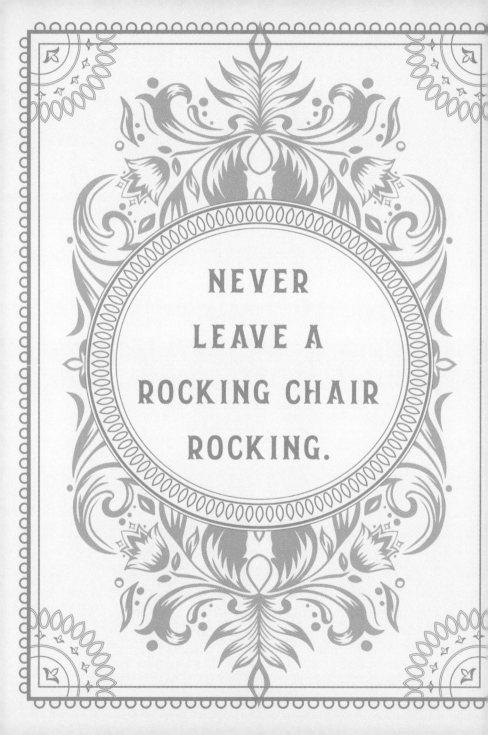

NEVER
LEAVE A
ROCKING CHAIR
ROCKING.

SOUTHERNERS THINK THAT IF YOU LEAVE AN empty rocking chair rocking, you are inviting the dark spirits to come and sit down for an unwanted visit. In the land of large covered porches, you will always find plenty of rocking chairs. Next time you're on the porch and get up to refill your cocktail, make sure you don't leave your rocking chair rocking.

A BOTTLE TREE IN SOMEONE'S YARD IS A COMMON SIGHT in the South. According to African folk legend, the glass bottles were able to lure evil spirits, also called haints, that came out at night, capturing them in the bottles so they couldn't enter the house. The sound made when the wind blows through the necks of the bottles is thought to be the captured evil spirits howling from within. In the morning, the sun would destroy the trapped spirits. The tree itself is usually a decorative piece of metal rods shaped like a tree with the branches holding the bottles. My parents had one in their yard filled with around twenty bottles of different colors. The dark-blue and bright-red bottles were said to possess magical qualities, for spirits were believed to be drawn to these colors in particular.

These bottles can hold more than just a drink.

Here's to
a new start
on old
habits.

SOUTHERNERS START THE YEAR WITH A MULTITUDE of superstitions thought to bring good luck in the upcoming new year. First, you are not to wash or clean or really do any work on New Year's Day, so you must do it before. The thought is that cleaning or doing the laundry will sweep or wash away any good luck you will have in the upcoming year. Second, while you should not work on New Year's Day, cooking is allowed. The traditional Southern New Year's Day spread consists of pork, black-eyed peas, collard greens, and cornbread. Black-eyed peas and collard greens, usually both cooked with bacon, symbolize luck in money while cornbread and pork symbolize gold and prosperity, respectively. It is also favored to eat pork over chicken on New Year's Day because pigs root forward and chickens scratch backward.

A PURSE ON THE FLOOR MEANS MONEY OUT THE door. A Southern lady's bag should never be placed on the floor for it indicates a purse that holds no real value. If you place your bag on the floor, even if by accident, it could bring bad luck in the form of financial distress.

YOU BETTA
NOT SET THAT
PURSE ON
THE FLOOR.

The baby made me eat it.

THERE ARE MANY SOUTHERN SUPERSTITIONS
about pregnancy and one of the most popular is that eating spicy food and having heartburn gives the baby lots of hair. With all the spicy food in the South, all babies should be coming into the world with mop tops of hair, but that is not the case. We know women usually have more heartburn than usual during pregnancy, but it has very little to do with their little one's hair growth. Spicy food is also thought to bring on labor, and this does seem to have more truth to it. I didn't crave a lot of spicy food when I was pregnant the first time, but the last time I did, it brought on labor. My son was not born with a lot of hair, but he's been a spicy, active kid since birth!

SPILLING SALT IS CONSIDERED TO BE BAD LUCK and caused by the devil. It's long been used in many cartoons of an angel on your right shoulder and the devil on your left. Throwing salt over your left shoulder is thought to blind the devil and reverse the bad luck that may be coming your way. It is also considered bad luck to pass someone salt at the dinner table. In doing so, you're passing along sorrow. Next time you sit down to eat and someone asks for the salt, place the shaker close enough for them to reach and pick it up themselves. That way, everyone at the table remains in good luck and fortune.

KEEP CALM AND PASS THE SALT.

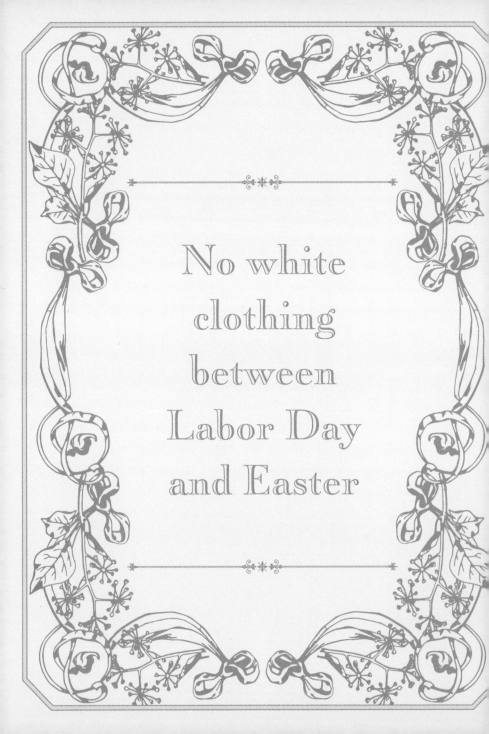

No white
clothing
between
Labor Day
and Easter

IN THE NINETEENTH-CENTURY IN THE SOUTH, BEFORE
everyone had the treasured air-conditioning we love
today, people wore white and light-colored clothing
usually made of thinner fabrics such as linen to keep
cool. It was thought that those who wore white clothing
were from a more affluent upper class and used it to
distinguish themselves from the working class. If you
wore darker colors in the summer months, it was to
hide the dirt and grime from a long day's work. Easter is
usually when we break out our favorite white clothing.

While many people still keep to this rule, fashion and social
graces have changed in present days, so it is not uncommon to
see people wearing white past Labor Day. They will, however,
receive the ever-popular "Bless your heart" if they do.

HAVING ITCHY PALMS IS THOUGHT TO mean that you will soon gain or lose money. Here's the trick: Money is coming your way if your right palm itches, but if it's the left, you stand to lose some soon. It is also very important to know you shouldn't scratch the itch. If you do, you could stop that money from coming to you. The only sure fire way to scratch the itch without sacrificing your financial future is to rub your palm on a very old piece of wood. I've personally heard this superstition for as long as I can remember. I'd scratch my hand and inevitably someone would say, "Oh, money is coming!"

Oh,
money
is
coming!

Hold your breath!

• • ● • •

THE THOUGHT IS THAT IF YOU ARE HOLDING your breath, the spirits cannot enter your body. This is a superstition I remember vividly learning as a child. Back in elementary school, our bus driver would shout, "Hold your breath!" as we passed several graveyards. Apparently, it wasn't just to make a bus full of children quiet down.

• • ● • •

HAVE YOU EVER WALKED THROUGH A PARKING LOT, spotted a coin, and reached to grab it? Well, from now on you better check to make sure you're not picking it up if it's tails! A coin tails up means bad luck is coming your way. If this happens, you are to pick up the penny and lay it back down heads up to give luck to the next person who comes its way. If you come across a penny heads up, pick it up but never spend it. Keep it with you to bring you good luck. This is a superstition that I personally partake in along with my entire family and even my children.

Never
pick up a
coin if
it's tails up.

CAREFUL
YOU'RE NOT
ACCIDENTALLY
CUTTING TIES.

KNIVES CAN BE IMPORTANT FAMILY HEIRLOOMS and highly collectible works of art and craftsmanship. It is believed that in giving a knife the giver loses their power, and that the knife's blade cuts the ties between the giver and the receiver. To prevent this from happening, the recipient of the knife must trade a coin of any value. The use of the coin ensures that the bond between the two people isn't severed and that power isn't given away without compensation. Some people place a coin in the box just in case the recipient doesn't have one on hand. Before my wedding, my aunt gave my husband and I two beautiful sets of stainless-steel steak knives. After opening the gift, both she and my mother made sure I handed over two coins, one for each set.

THIS SUPERSTITION IS VERY PARTICULAR TO my family in Southern Louisiana. (I had to add it in this book simply because my husband finds it ridiculous.) In my family, guests are always welcome. However, when you leave, you have to exit from the door you entered. If you came in through the front door, you leave by the front door, even if the party is held on the back porch and there's a side gate. It is believed that in doing this you take all the luck that is in the household with you. As a proper guest, you should always be respectful and leave things exactly as you found them, even if you can't necessarily see them. Some people say this superstition is more Irish folklore and it may be, but it's a tradition I've grown up with and still use today, much to my husband's dismay.

Lagniappe Luck

The term *lagniappe* means "a little extra" in the South. Here is a list of lesser-known superstitions to learn about and perhaps bring you good luck in life.

• • • • •

1. **No haint blue ceilings?** If you can't repaint your porch ceiling haint blue, a child's handprint in blue on the porch will work to keep the spirits away.

2. **Come on in!** The first guest you welcome into your home at the beginning of the new year will determine the year for your household. For good luck, have your first guest be a tall and dark-haired man.

3. **Mirrors are a doorway.** When someone dies, all the mirrors in the house must be covered so that the spirit doesn't get trapped in them and can go on into the afterlife.

4. **A lady's first pearl.** Wearing pearls on your wedding day will bring harmony to marriage.

5. **The best hair-washing day.** Wash your hair with the first rain of May to bring good luck.

6. **An even dinner table.** Never invite thirteen people to dinner; it will bring bad luck to one of the guests.

7. **Eat your greens!** Eat raw okra for good luck.

8. **Save the ends for last.** Never eat the ends of the bread before eating the middle or you will not be able to make ends meet.

9. **Animals can sense the weather.** If cows are lying down in the field, rain is coming.

10. **Is it cold in here?** If you get a sudden and unexpected chill, someone is walking over your grave.

11. **Need a broom?** Always buy a new broom when you move, so you do not bring old dirt with you.

12. **Keep your hat on your head.** Never put your hat on the bed. Hats were placed on coffins a long time ago, so doing this now is thought to bring bad luck.

13. **Good luck is everywhere.** Hanging a horseshoe over your door with its ends pointed up is believed to catch good luck for those who live in the home. If you hang it with its ends pointing down, you will share good luck with all those who pass through. So, choose how you want to share your luck!

Southern Dictionary

O ur specific Southern words are very
colorful and imaginative. They are
an important part of our past and present
culture. These unique words and phrases are
used every day to spice up our conversations,
just like how spices enhance our food. Use
this chapter to prepare for chatting with us
when you come for a visit. The better you
understand our unique linguistic lagniappe,
the better you can appreciate being a
Southerner yourself.

ACCENT: Southern accents are traditionally known as slow and very drawn out. Vowel sounds lengthen to create a laid-back, rhythmic cadence. Accents vary depending on the state where they are spoken.

BAYOU: A bayou is a slow-moving creek and swampy area of a river or lake. The word *bayou* comes from the Louisiana French and is thought to originate from the Choctaw word *bayuk*, which means "small stream." They are filled with cypress trees draped in Spanish moss, which makes them the perfect setting of many stories in the South, whether love or scary stories.

BISCUITS: It is a belief that biscuits go with pretty much every meal in the South. They are fluffy, flaky, and filled with countless memories of family and friends gathered around the dining table. Biscuits are made with a type of flour ground from soft wheat, which grows readily in the South due to the warm and humid climate. Every Southerner swears by the staple of Lily White Flour when making their biscuits.

BOUND TO: "Bound to" is the simple Southern abbreviation used when you are sure something will happen or you're going to make it happen.

BOURBON: Bourbon is a type of American whiskey, distilled from a mash made primarily of corn, and it must be stored in charred oak barrels. Bourbon is also the featured spirit in many famous cocktail recipes, from the old-fashioned to the mint julep.

CADDYWAMPUS: This funny sounding word is a favorite descriptive word for many. When you use it, you're telling the listener that what you're describing is all out of whack; it's askew or crooked.

CAJUNS: The Cajun people are descendants of French-speaking Roman Catholics, who were exiled out of Acadia in Canada after they refused to pledge allegiance to the British crown. Their expulsion was known as Le Grand Dérangement, and they settled in Southern Louisiana. Cajun is also used in Louisiana as a broad term when referring to the southeastern part of the state called Acadiana. Cajuns believe in strong family relationships, good food, and fun celebrations filled with music.

CANE SYRUP: Cane syrup is made from raw, pressed cane juice that's boiled down so it's a darker color. It has a rich flavor of dark sugar and rum. Southerners love to drizzle it on their pancakes and waffles, and even when cooking meats, mixing cocktails, and baking desserts. In the South, Steen's Cane Syrup is the staple in our kitchens.

CAST IRON: Cast-iron cookware is handed down just as often as a grandmother's silver or pearls. Using this treasured cookware is not for the faint of heart. It must be hand-washed, seasoned, oiled, and loved. However, investing in good cookware means it can be used for almost every meal and will last for generations.

COME SEE: "Come see" is a shorthand expression meaning "come and see" or "come here." It is primarily used in the lower part of the South, closer to the coast. I grew up saying "come see" and never realized it was such a localized phrase until I met my husband.

CORNBREAD: Southern cornbread differs from its Northern version, as Southerners do not use sugar. Instead, we use a different type of cornmeal and add buttermilk. It's also most often cooked in a cast-iron skillet, resulting in a golden, warm treat just waiting to be slathered in butter and paired with a cold glass of milk.

COTTON: Cotton fabric is soft and cool, and its breathable fibers make it a favorite of Southern seamstresses. Cotton fibers can also hold twenty-four times their weight, which makes it perfect for heavy, humid temperatures.

DINNER AND SUPPER: There is quite the confusion when it comes to which meal is which, so let's set it straight. Dinner is the main meal of the day, to be eaten at midday back when people worked mainly from home on their local farms. Supper was a lighter meal, eaten at night after a hard day's work. However, in modern times, the language has been reversed with supper being the midday meal and dinner the night because people mainly work away from their home and are on the go during the day.

DOUBLE FIRST NAMES: Double first names are so popular in the South because of our extensive family ties and because we're all stubborn. A husband and wife usually compromise using two names for their children to honor both sides of the family that are so important to them. Double names also roll off the slow Southern tongue a whole lot easier.

EAT UP WITH: When we say someone is eat up with, it means they are all consumed with it, such as jealousy, anger, or just an overall bad mood. It's also pronounced "Et up."

ÉTOUFFÉE: Étouffée is a comfort food dish from Cajun cuisine made from a light roux and served over rice, featuring seafood such as crab, shrimp, and the all-star crawfish. The word means "smothered" and that's just what it is: yummy stewed toppings over warm white rice.

FIT AS A FIDDLE: Considering the Southern diet, you would think that this is a phrase Southerners wouldn't use much, but we do. When you say someone is fit as a fiddle, it means they are healthy and strong.

FIT TO BE TIED: Using this phrase is the ultimate expression of anger. Southerners love dramatic talk, and if you are so angry, you'd need to be tied up. That's intense!

FIXIN' TO: Fixin' to is one of the most famous Southern phrases. When someone tells you they are fixin' to do something, they mean it's going to happen, but there is no set timeline, so grab a glass of sweet tea and just hold your horses while you're at it.

FLEUR-DE-LIS: With French heritage, fleur-de-lis means "lily flower." The fleur-de-lis has long been associated as a symbol of the South, especially the city of New Orleans. It's been used to represent royalty and power, the French cultural heritage, and Christianity. Of course, it's another important symbol of the South, football, and the New Orleans Saints football team.

GIMME SOME SUGAR: Every Southern child has heard this expression more times than they can count. Gimme some sugar simply means give me a kiss, plant a wet one on me, show me some love!

GINGHAM: The term *gingham* is believed to have originated in the seventeenth-century from the Malay word *genggang*, meaning striped or checkered. This beloved fabric is always printed on cotton, perfect for our hot temperatures, and favored in many colors for apparel, textiles, and even home décor.

GOOD OLE BOY: Hopefully you know your fair share of good ole boys. They are known for loyalty, fellowship, and all kinds of boisterous good ole fun!

GRAVY: Country, milk, sausage, brown, sawmill, and white. There are many names for the yummy gravy goodness that tops rice, biscuits, and mashed potatoes all across the South. Each recipe holds different flavors and ingredients perfect for each and every meal.

GUSSIED UP: Getting gussied up is a sign a good time is about to be had. Whether you're making yourself more fancy with clothes or your home with new paint or furniture in time for a party, gussied up can make everything more interesting.

HOLD YOUR HORSES: The idiom means to wait, be patient, or to slow down. In 1843, it was written as "hold your hosses."

Hoss was the common slang term for horse at the time. In September of 1844, the *Picayune* in New Orleans printed, "Oh, hold your hosses, Squire. There's no use gettin' riled, no how."

HOWDY: A form of hello, how do you do, how are you. Usually it's accompanied with a nod, a tip of the hat, or a two-finger salute.

HUMIDITY: The Southern states are known for being some of the most humid areas in the country. Their subtropical climate creates hot and humid summers with lots of rain and mild winters. Humidity also helps produce the lush landscape of the South and its residents' "glowing" skin.

ICED TEA: Every Southerner has their own unique recipe for making their version of sweet tea. It's really quite simple: Use large batches of freshly brewed black tea, sweeten while piping hot, and serve over ice. Be sure to keep it chilled in the fridge, so you'll be the ultimate hostess offering a glass when company comes to visit.

IRIS: The iris is a favorite flower of the South. It comes in a wide variety of colors. Its deep symbolism and fleur-de-lis shape makes it worthy of Mardi Gras royalty, krewes, and being the muse for artists from the French Quarter to the Florida Keys.

JAMBALAYA: Jambalaya comes from the Provençal word *jambalaia* meaning mix-up, and that's exactly what this delicious entrée is: a mix of rice, meat, and the Holy Trinity. It's a long-standing favorite in kitchens and restaurants across the South with two distinct versions of Cajun, which is meat- and veggie-based, and Creole, which has tomatoes.

JAZZ: The original American musical jazz originated in New Orleans with roots in the blues, ragtime, African rhythms, and European musical concepts. Jazz is the heartbeat of Southern life, from beginning to end at jazz funerals.

JAZZ FUNERAL: Even in death, Southerners love to party. A jazz funeral is a time-honored tradition of celebrating a person's life with music, dancing, and a parade to the graveyard through the streets.

JULEP: A mint julep is a bourbon- and mint-based cocktail honored at the Kentucky Derby and served in silver-tapered cups called Julep cups.

JUNIOR LEAGUE: The South may be filled with ole boys' clubs, but there is a very important one for women that reigns supreme, called the Junior League. The "League" is a volunteer organization of women who help their communities through multiple fundraisers and events. There are social aspects to the Junior League, but overall, the women who make up the organization have a purpose to better their communities each and every day.

KENTUCKY DERBY: The first weekend of May more than 150,000 people gather under the Twin Spires at Churchill Downs in their finest afternoon attire and fascinators to watch one of the most prestigious horse races in the world, a.k.a. the

Kentucky Derby. The owner of the winning horse receives a gold trophy, the only one presented in major American sports.

KEY LIME PIE: This classic Southern dessert takes its name from the key limes from Florida in the original recipe. Unfortunately, key limes have not been grown commercially in the United States since a hurricane devastated Miami, Florida, back in 1926.

KREWE: A twist of the word *crew*, this is a group of people who coordinates parades such as Mardi Gras, or festivities or events for a carnival celebration. Krewes are most often associated with Mardi Gras parades. The term was coined by The Mistick Krewe of Comus in 1857.

LAGNIAPPE: Lagniappe simply means "a little extra." It can be a free gift with purchase from a store or something given out of generosity.

LIVE OAKS: Live oaks are magical symbols of the South. These evergreen iconic trees and their twisty branches have graced the soil for many, many years, creating the inspiration for famous paintings and poems.

LIVIN'/WALKIN' IN HIGH COTTON: The South as a whole is much more rural than other areas of the United States. Farming and weather are very important aspects of the culture, so a lot of the popular terms deal with such. High cotton refers to the tall and healthy cotton plants. These types of plants were very profitable, so when you say someone is "walkin' in high cotton," that means they are doing well for themselves whether financially or socially.

MAGNOLIA: The magnolia is the most beautiful and well-known flower in all of the South. This perennial tree that blooms in spring and summer can grow from 60 to 80 feet (18 to 24 m) tall. It inspires all who see them with its tight buds that eventually bloom into magnificent white flowers with an intoxicating smell.

MAKIN' GROCERIES: Makin' groceries is an old New Orleans saying with French origins that means "to buy groceries." It is a rough translation from the French phrase *faire son marche*, that means to do or to make grocery shopping.

MARDI GRAS: Mardi Gras has quite a complicated history and many ways to celebrate it in the South. Believe it or not, Mardi Gras started in Mobile, Alabama, not New Orleans, Louisiana, where it has become synonymous. Mardi Gras also takes on a more country vibe in the western part of Louisiana where the Cajun residents chase chickens from home to home to create a community gumbo. It also brings out countless cinnamon cakes covered in purple, green, and gold icing, elegant balls and parties celebrating the royalty, and more beads and throws than you could count or carry.

MASON JARS: In 1858, John Landis Mason patented a threaded screw-top glass jar that is airtight and watertight. Mason jars serve many purposes: Fill them with your favorite cocktail, use it as a candleholder, have it hold a freshly picked flower arrangement, or pickle or store veggies inside.

NASHVILLE HOT CHICKEN: Nashville is not just famous for music. Legend has it that this spicy fried chicken dish was actually created by accident. The originator, Prince's Hot Chicken Shack, was purportedly a womanizer, and his girlfriend at the time cooked him a fried chicken breakfast with extra pepper as revenge for stepping out with someone who was not her. Her plot backfired. He loved the chicken, and the rest is history.

NATCHEZ: High on the bluffs, the Jewel of the Mississippi is filled with beautiful antebellum homes, churches, and countless historic buildings. Natchez is also the namesake for the Natchez Trace, a 444-mile (715 km) path from Natchez to Nashville, Tennessee.

NEKID: Everyone was born naked, but when you have no clothes on and you're up to no good . . . you're nekid!

NEW ORLEANS: Louis Armstrong famously said, "Do you know what it means to miss New Orleans?" New Orleans is a city that creeps into the souls of those who visit. The cuisine, music, architecture, culture, festivals, and attitude stay with you if you leave. The unofficial motto of the city is *laissez les bon temps rouler*, meaning "let the good times roll," and this is something New Orleans does well.

NICKNAMES: Nicknames can be as common to people as their given names. Sometimes they can be a shortened version of the actual name, a description of the person (for example, "He's so sweet, we call him Shug"), or just for the fun of having a crazy name that makes no sense except to the family that bestows it.

NUTRIA: Have you ever heard the expression "so ugly it's cute"? Well, that is the perfect description of the nutria rat. Venture into any Louisiana swamp and you're sure to come across one of these giant, hairy, overgrown rats with big yellow teeth.

OKRA: Fried okra may be the ever-popular side item or appetizer, but okra is known for much more. This slimy Southern favorite is a natural thickener in soups and gumbos. One popular way to prepare okra is cooked with diced tomatoes, your favorite smoked meat of choice, and served over a bowl of white rice.

OLD-FASHIONED: If you want to drink like a true Southerner, the old-fashioned is the best place to start. This whiskey-based cocktail got its name in the late 1800s when bartenders began experimenting more and making more complicated cocktails. Patrons began longing for simpler drinks and began asking for favorite "old-fashioned" cocktails. The old-fashioned is made by muddling sugar and water with bitters, whiskey, or rye bourbon, and garnished with an orange slice and a cocktail cherry. It's served over ice in a rocks glass otherwise known as an old-fashioned glass.

OYSTERS: Oysters can be eaten raw, smoked, chargrilled, baked, fried, roasted, stewed, canned, pickled, or even in a cocktail shooter. There are hundreds of varieties of oysters harvested across the South of different flavors, textures, and sizes. The old rule is that the best time of year for oysters is when there is an "r" in the month (September to April). There is nothing better to most Southerners than a huge platter of freshly shucked oysters sitting on a bed of ice, neatly served with lemon wedges, saltine crackers, and a spicy cocktail sauce. Some oyster purists believe no accompaniments are needed except maybe your grandmother's sterling silver oyster fork. Others throw a quick dash of Tabasco hot sauce on and slurp it down. The most important rule is to slow down, enjoy the experience, and come back for more.

PEACHES: Peaches are Georgia's namesake fruit. Atlanta has over seventy streets with peach in the name, so it can get quite confusing for a tourist. The state's weather and perfect red clay soil are thought to help make their peaches oh so sweet. After the Civil War, Southern farmers started growing peaches instead of cotton as a way to help rebrand and rebuild the South. Peaches are the quintessential summer fruit and can be eaten fresh, baked, or even grilled for use in savory dishes.

PECANS: Pecans, from the hickory family, are the only tree indigenous to the southern part of the United States. A slave named Antoine on the Oak Alley Plantation in Louisiana is credited with grafting the first pecan tree. Pecan harvest ranges from October to December, so it's no wonder pecan pie is one of the favorite holiday desserts.

PICKLING: Instead of letting fruit or vegetables go bad in the kitchen, Southerners used their creativity and a trusty mason jar. With a simple brining recipe, asparagus, beets, bell peppers, cabbage, cauliflower, carrots, cucumbers, eggs, green beans, mushrooms, onions, peaches, squash, tomatoes, and even watermelon are saved and start a new pickled life. Brining recipes are a simple mixture of vinegar, water, sugar, salt, and your favorite spices.

PIDDLIN': Piddlin' means to spend your time in a wasteful manner, dawdling around and really doing nothing of any importance with your day. We affectionately refer to my father as "The Piddler." He earned this nickname by sweeping the garage ten times or raking the gravel in the garden walks to be just perfect. We even went so far as to have seven T-shirts made up, one in a different color for each day of the week, with his nickname.

PIROGUE: A pirogue is a long, small, narrow boat made from a single tree trunk. Cajuns in Louisiana typically used cypress trees. This shallow boat easily maneuvers through the swamp and marshland.

QUEENS: The ultimate goal of any Southern woman in a Mardi Gras krewe is to be crowned queen. A new queen is selected each year late in the fall to reign over the upcoming Mardi Gras season. The Krewe votes, and the king and queen do not need to be related to each other. It is a huge honor to be chosen and the queen spends her season attending and hosting parties and riding in one of the first floats in the parade, where she is decked out in a sparkling dress with an ornate train and collar.

RECKON: I reckon I'll have to explain how to use this word properly. Reckon is just a simple term meaning to think or suppose something or to believe it's true.

RED BEANS: Red beans and rice is the traditional dish served on Mondays in the South, specifically in Louisiana. The story goes that the ham bone leftover from Sunday's dinner was used to flavor a big pot of red kidney beans along with spices, onions, and bell peppers. The pot could be left to cook all day while the laundry was being done. Even today, red beans and rice is still served at many local restaurants and even schools. New Orleans's own Louis Armstrong loved the dish so much that he used to famously sign his letters, Red Beans and Ricely Yours.

ROUX: A roux is an important staple in the Southern kitchen. It's a cooked mix of equal parts flour and fat used to thicken sauces and stews. Mastering a roux takes time, practice, and patience. Burning it is a horrible, stinky experience no one wants to have because you'll never forget the smell, and like any upstanding Southern chef, you certainly will not admit to ever having burned it. A little white lie never hurt anyone ...

RUCKUS: A traditional definition of a ruckus is a noisy commotion. A ruckus also can be when that possum you thought was playing dead runs into your house or when Uncle Shug has one to many sips of the rye whiskey. As you can imagine, when a ruckus is caused, it's loud, noisy, confusing, and usually the cause of stories to be told year after year.

RYE: Rye is a grass grown as a grain to be used in bread, beer, and, most importantly, whiskey. By law, rye whiskey is to be made from a mash of at least 51 percent rye, distilled at no more than 160 US proof, and aged in charred, new oak barrels.

With the rise of the craft cocktail, rye whiskey is making a comeback in the United States. The top choice cocktail using rye whiskey is also a Southern one and known as the first ever cocktail, the Sazerac.

SAZERAC: The Sazerac holds the distinction of being credited as the first cocktail recognized by name. Created in New Orleans in the mid-1800s, it's a favorite to this day in the South and for good reason. This sipping cocktail is a strong mix of flavors perfect for a summer day spent on the porch.

SEERSUCKER: Seersucker is the perfect fabric. This thin fabric is woven in such a way that it causes some threads to bunch together, giving the fabric a puckered texture. This unevenness causes the fabric to be held away from the wearer's skin. In the heat of the summer, the skin is allowed to breathe rather than being stuck with wet, sweaty fabric. In 1909, famed New Orleans clothier Joseph Haspel Sr. brought seersucker fabric to men's suits. These suits were so much more comfortable because of their ease of wear and the fact they didn't need ironing. Seersucker is so popular in the South that June 13 is proclaimed as National Seersucker Day!

SHINDIG: Ready to celebrate, dance, and have a good ole time? That's the perfect definition of a shindig. There are so many people having a good time and dancing that you literally get kicked in the shins!

SKEETER: A skeeter is an annoying little insect, also known as the state mascot to many, the mosquito. Skeeter can also be a nickname, a term of endearment for a busy little energetic person who flits around just like a mosquito.

SLAW: Coleslaw is a cabbage salad and cabbage is the only consistent ingredient in this recipe. Southerners make their coleslaw with mustard, vinegar, or even mayonnaise. One thing also remains certain: coleslaw is the perfect topping to any BBQ sandwich.

SNO-BALL: In the South, we call this fluffy summertime treat a sno-ball. Sno-balls are actually different from snow cones and the difference is all in the ice. Snow cones use dense, crunchy ice. We finely shave our ice and then top it with flavored cane syrups. The shaved ice absorbs the syrups better, making for an evenly flavored consistency. Sno-balls are frequently topped with evaporated milk or stuffed with ice cream.

STOMPIN' GROUNDS: Your favorite place, the place where you grew up and you know every inch, that is your stompin' ground. It's a place near and dear to your heart.

TABASCO: Tabasco is a Louisiana hot sauce made from a secret recipe of special tabasco peppers, vinegar, and salt. Created more than 150 years ago on Avery Island by the McIlhenny Company, Tabasco is famous all around the world and the favorite topping to many dishes and meals.

TACKY: When someone is considered tacky, they are showing behavior that is thought to be lacking class or in poor taste. Wearing white after Labor Day is one of the tackiest things you can do. The only proper way to deal with a tacky person is to say "bless your heart" and wish them well.

TOMATO PIE: You might think a tomato pie sounds strange, but this savory dish has been a comfort food for ages in the South. Tomato pie is best made when summer tomatoes are at their peak and most ripe. The pie is made from a pie shell, filled with tomatoes, spices, and shredded cheese mixed with mayonnaise and baked until a golden brown.

TUCKERED OUT: Spend too much time in the garden, working the church bazaar, or chasing your children around the yard, you'll be simply tuckered out. Sometimes the word *plum* is added to this phrase and that just means you're really tired!

UMPTEEN: When the number is so large, you use the word *umpteen* because there is just no other way to describe it.

UNIVERSITY (SEC schools and football): Now this may make our Southern football fans sound uppity, but we believe with all our heart, the SEC universities are the best and we can prove it. SEC universities put a lot of money into athletics and the talent they recruit, and with that they create excellence on and off the field. SEC schools have won more national championships in all areas of athletics.

UPPITY: When someone acts uppity, they think they are better than someone else. These people are just outright unpleasant like a patty in a cow pasture.

VERANDA: Verandas came to be in the South as a way to adapt to the very hot summers, high humidity, and the need to sit for a spell and visit. Verandas are usually primary-floor covered structures and open air on three sides. The purpose is to provide shelter from the sun while allowing the cross breeze. Most verandas also can have as much furniture outside as they do on the inside to provide comfortable seating for visits and cool cocktails.

VIEUX CARRÉ: Vieux carré has two meanings: a historic area and a cocktail. In French it translates to "old square" and describes the famous New Orleans French Quarter neighborhood. The famous cocktail was created in the French Quarter in 1938 by Walter Bergeron, the head bartender at the Hotel Monteleone. The cocktail is the New Orleans version of the Manhattan. It uses rye whiskey, cognac, Peychaud's and Angostura bitters, and Benedictine. Take a trip to New Orleans and have a spin at the Carousel Bar and enjoy one yourself.

VINEGAR: Southerners have found a multitude of uses for vinegar, from scrubbing floors to medicinal uses, but the most important in the hot South is as a preservative. Southerners acclimated to the taste so well that it's very common in restaurants to find bottles of pepper-infused vinegar.

WHISKEY: Whiskey is a favorite type of liquor made from fermented grain mash and aged in wooden casks made of charred white oak. American whiskey must be distilled to no more than 80 percent alcohol by volume and barreled at no more than 125 proof. Whiskey is the liquor of choice for many famous Southern cocktails.

WORN SLAP OUT: While tuckered out is tired, worn slap out is not just physically tired, but mentally tired as well. It's the end all be all of tired in the South.

WROUGHT IRON: Wrought iron is to a building like decorative lace is to clothing. This particular metal is favored by blacksmiths for its durability, ease of use, and resistance to corrosion. It is created by repeatedly heating and reworking cast iron with the utmost skill, creating twists and swirls and decorative forms. Sadly, wrought iron is no longer produced on a commercial scale, but it is still made for replication and restoration of historical properties. Ornamental work today described as wrought iron is actually made of mild steel.

Y'ALL AND ALL Y'ALL: Y'all is the abbreviation for "you all." Y'all can be singular or plural really, but when you say "all y'all," you mean a lot more than two. All y'all usually refers to a group, and most usually a family.

YANKEE: This is a well-used phrase in the South. We refer to Yankees as our Northern friends who live above the Mason-Dixon Line. It can also refer to folks in the western part of the United States as well. The word is not quite as derogatory as it was right after the Civil War.

YARD BIRD: This should be an easy word to understand: What birds roam around your yard? Why chickens of course! This term originated in the South due to homeowners allowing chickens to roam free in their front yards and on the property.

YONDER: Yonder is a directional term in the South. "Where are you going?" "I'm going up yonder." To anyone else, they would still question where, but to Southerners, we know exactly where yonder is.

ZAPP'S: You can't go to any grocery or gas station in the South and not see the Zapp's potato chips and the famous logo. Their slogan is "daringly different", and they mean it! Zapp's has flavors ranging from crawfish flavor and Creole onion to more classics such as dill pickle and BBQ.

ZATARAIN'S: Zatarain's is a Louisiana company that makes seasonings and meal mixes with a Creole and Cajun flair. They are most famous for their crab boil in the iconic yellow packaging.

ZYDECO: Zydeco is an up-tempo music style that was created in rural Southwest Louisiana in the area called Cajun Country. It blends blues, rock and roll, soul, R&B, Cajun, and early Creole music. The musicians feature an accordion and a Creole washboard called the frottoir.

Conclusion

    —— ✦ ★ ✦ ——

It was such an honor to be asked to write this book about the South. I would like to say I learned a lot in doing so, but that was not the case. I think the correct description of my time with this book is that I reaffirmed things instead of learned new things. Thinking back on all the stories, phrases, and descriptions I grew up with was so heartwarming, even the times I received a *bless your heart* myself. This unique place has given me such a special upbringing and so many stories to tell. Thinking back on stories from my family and all the unique tidbits and traditions is truly something to be valued. I'm proud to say I was raised in the South. It has had an influence on my personality, my business projects, and my individual style and mission in life.

It's a joy to spread what the South means to me through this book and to share the things that make us unique. My hope is that this appreciation comes across to you. Some traditions may seem strange, but the root of everything is family and community. Like it says on page 222, our lives revolve around good food, family, and sitting and taking the time with the ones you love. I hope this book encourages you to make small talk with the next stranger you meet, make your own pot of gumbo, and have a get-together to experience new tastes and cultures. Just like our seasonings, we may be too strong for some and that's OK. We'll still welcome you back with a smile, a handshake, a cocktail, and a bowl of jambalaya.

References

"American Pastime Cocktails: Mint Julep and Old Fashioned." *Institute of Culinary Education*, March 6, 2017. https://www.ice.edu/blog/american-pastime-cocktails-mint-julep-and-old-fashioned?_gl=1%2A1l373aa%2A_gcl_au%2AMTg2MjA2MjgyNS4xNzI3Mjk1ODY5%2A_ga%2AOTUyOTAxMDQyLjE3MjcyOTU4Njk.%2A_ga_MBTGG7KX5Y%2AMTcyNzI5NTg2OC4xLjEuMTcyNzI5NzYyNC4wLjAuMA.

Carroll, David. "Drunker than Cooter Brown." *JCSentinel*, December 2, 2022. https://jcsentinel.com/feature_story/article_8a9caeb0-7290-11ed-a5f7-6f2c29736b1c.html.

Churchill, Abbye. "An Illustrated History of Cocktails in the South." *Kitchn*. Apartment Therapy, LLC., May 11, 2016. https://www.thekitchn.com/an-illustrated-history-of-cocktails-in-the-south-230513.

Darrisaw, Michelle. "What's the Difference Between Dinner and Supper?" *Southern Living*, 2017. https://www.southernliving.com/culture/supper-vs-dinner#:~:text=Merriam%2DWebster%20establishes%20dinner%20as.

Dutton, Jill. "Everything You Want to Know about Pecans." 10Best. *USA TODAY*, June 27, 2020. https://10best.usatoday.com/interests/food-culture/pecans-101-what-to-know-about-southern-nut/#.

Flynn, Richard. "'Hold Your Horses' Meaning." UsingEnglish.com. 2024. https://www.usingenglish.com/reference/idioms/hold+your+horses.html.

"Gumbo Cookoff." Greater Iberia Chamber of Commerce. July 25, 2024. https://www.iberiachamber.org/gumbo-cookoff/.

Landon, Grelun, and Irwin Stambler. *Country Music: The Encyclopedia*. St. Martin's Press, 2000.

Love, Melany. "If You See a Blue Porch Ceiling, This Is What It Means." *Taste of Home*, July 20, 2021. https://www.tasteofhome.com/article/blue-porch-ceiling-meaning/#:~:text=Gullah%20folklore%20explains%20that%20.

Martin, Mackenzie. "Meet Henry Perry, the Black Entrepreneur Who Created Kansas City Barbecue in the Early 1900s." KCUR - Kansas City News and NPR. February 13, 2021. https://www.kcur.org/arts-life/2021-02-13/kansas-city-barbecue-bbq-henry-perry-gates-arthur-bryants-history.

Nott, Marty. "Rye." *The Libation Lounge,* April 7, 2024. https://libationlounge.com/tag/rye/?_gl=1%2A403v9l%2A_gcl_au%2AMTg2MjA2MjgyNS4xNzI3Mjk1ODY5%2A_ga%2AOTUyOTAxMDQyLjE3MjcyOTU4Njk.%2A_ga_MBTGG7KX5Y%2AMTcyNzI5NTg2OC4xLjEuMTcyNzI5NzIzOS4wLjAuMA.

"Seersucker Facts for Kids." Seersucker Facts for Kids. Accessed September 25, 2024. https://kids.kiddle.co/Seersucker?_gl=1%2Agae7pc%2A_gcl_au%2AMTg2MjA2MjgyNS4xNzI3Mjk1ODY5%2A_ga%2AOTUyOTAxMDQyLjE3MjcyOTU4Njk.%2A_ga_MBTGG7KX5Y%2AMTcyNzI5NTg2OC4xLjEuMTcyNzI5Nzc5OC4wLjAuMA.

"Shop Clothing for Women and Men | JMcLaughlin.com." JMcLaughlin. 2024. https://www.jmclaughlin.com/blog/style/the-history-of-gingham#https://duesouth.media/what-is-gingham-and-discover-how-it-became-a-southern-style-icon/#.

Wikipedia Foundation. "Bayou." July 27, 2024. https://en.wikipedia.org/wiki/Bayou#cite_note-2.

Wikipedia Foundation. "Don't Get above Your Raising." July 30, 2023. https://en.wikipedia.org/wiki/Don%27t_get_above_your_raising#~:text=%22Don.

Wikipedia Foundation. "Hot Chicken." February 10, 2024. https://en.wikipedia.org/wiki/Hot_chicken.

Wikipedia Foundation. "If the Good Lord's Willing and the Creek Don't Rise." May 31, 2024. https://en.wikipedia.org/wiki/If_the_Good_Lord%27s_Willing_and_the_Creek_Don%27t_Rise#~:text=JSTOR%20(April%202021)-.

About the Author

---- ❦ ★ ❧ ----

EMILY WELCH is a watercolor artist, potter, author, illustrator, and art teacher. Her artwork pays homage to the unique spirit of the places she's always called home. Raised in Baton Rouge and now living in Shreveport, Louisiana, with her husband, two children, and beloved dog, Magnolia II, she is also the creator of the brand Magnolia Creative Co., selling handmade pottery and custom watercolors and illustrations representing Southern lifestyle and spirit.

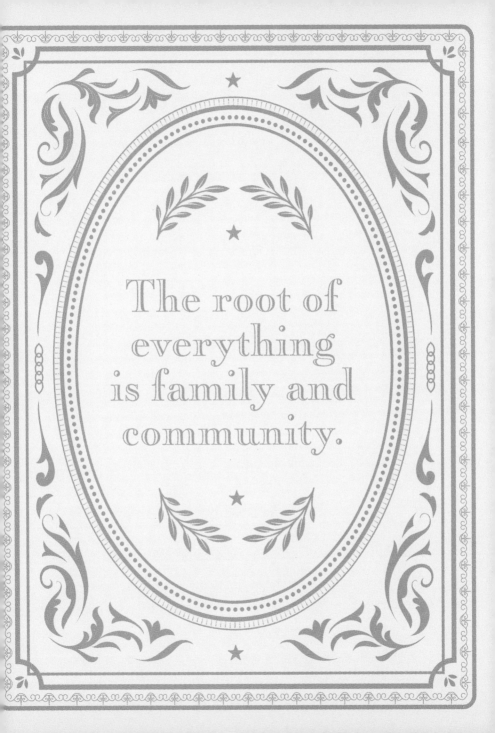

The root of
everything
is family and
community.

May you always enjoy good cooking and good eating, sitting, and sipping.

THESE WORDS COME FROM AN INSCRIPTION MY
grandmother wrote in a cookbook she gifted to my mother, and
the words my mother wrote to me in my copy of her published
cookbook. I am so happy to be able to continue the tradition.

First published in 2025 by Rock Point, an imprint of The Quarto Group,
142 West 36th Street, 4th Floor, New York, NY 10018, USA
(212) 779-4972 www.Quarto.com

Rock Point titles are also available at discount for retail, wholesale, promotional, and bulk purchase. For details, contact the Special Sales Manager by email at specialsales@quarto.com or by mail at The Quarto Group, Attn: Special Sales Manager, 100 Cummings Center Suite 265D, Beverly, MA 01915 USA.

10 9 8 7 6 5 4 3 2 1

ISBN: 978-1-57715-474-7

Digital edition published in 2025
eISBN: 978-0-7603-9286-7

Library of Congress Control Number: 2024951344

Group Publisher: Rage Kindelsperger
Editorial Director: Erin Canning
Creative Director: Laura Drew
Managing Editor: Cara Donaldson
Editor: Katelynn Abraham
Cover Design: Jo Obarowski
Interior Design: B. Middleworth

Printed in China